REAL WORLD TESTIMONIALS ABOUT HARNESSING YOUR TEAM'S COMPETITIVE ADVANTAGE THROUGH THE BEAUTY OF CONFLICT

"In an industry that has its roots in command and control, the concepts in this book provide a clear path for creating high-performing teams and a humane company culture. After having been first introduced to the Thrive! team seven years ago, I'm still getting great value from our work with Thrive! This is a must-read for any leader wanting to influence change on their team and in their organization overall."

Catharine Farrow
TMAC Resources CEO

"CrisMarie and Susan were instrumental in helping a 'smart' but 'unhealthy' team of mine work through some very serious, yet largely unspoken, conflicts. It wasn't a fast or easy process, but we're now the team that I knew we could be. The powerful techniques in *The Beauty of Conflict* had a huge impact on our teamwork and engagement—and we're having more fun and delivering even better results."

Mike Keller
Nationwide CIO

"I was introduced to CrisMarie and Susan when they came in to work with our leadership team at Microsoft. I really value their perspective on teams, conflict, .and building trust through vulnerability, curiosity and real-team work on business issues. I have reused their materials over and over to great success with leaders and teams. I'm thrilled that this book is now out for other leaders. Their style is real, personal and practical. It's a must-read for a leader wanting to build strong relationships and get great business results."

Kim Hardgraves
Microsoft Director, Business Operations & Compliance

"Who knew that growing up in a big Italian family full of conflict would provide me with the perfect training for business. . .an MBA at the dinner table! Susan and CrisMarie give us tools on how to embrace, bring out, use, and channel conflict to help teams get more out of each other and make better business decisions. This book is a must read for teams who want to be better together."

Pete Ungaro
Cray CEO

"We have been married nearly 25 years and in business together for even longer so clearly we've learned to 'manage' conflict. If not, we'd be either dead, divorced, or the business would have dissolved by now. We felt we had a good handle on this but after working with Susan and CrisMarie, we learned how to go beyond just managing conflict to actually harnessing the power (and the beauty!) of conflict to make our partnership—both personal and professional— even more powerful. Why settle for resolving conflict when you can turn it into a competitive advantage?"

Greg & Jenifer Lambert
TERRA Staffing Group, CEO and VP

"CrisMarie and Susan were critically important in the early formation of the leadership team at Theravance. The culture they helped create has transcended any particular employee at this point, and the company is thriving. I am thankful to them both. They've written an important book designed to help leaders break through the barriers of those inevitable personality clashes and leverage them for your team's competitive advantage."

Mathai Mammen
Global Head of Research and Development, Janssen Inc. Johnson & Johnson Company
Previously of Theravance, Senior Vice President Research and Development

"The Haven is a center for transformative learning dedicated to helping people build richer relationships with others and themselves. For more than 30 years we have offered programs in self responsible, relational living and the art and science of living well, together.

Susan and CrisMarie are The Haven's trusted team advisors, our go-to people to work with our board, management team, and staff. They have offered the highest quality team training at different times as teams have changed and grown, and especially as team members have got into difficulties with each other. Each time they leave the organization in better shape, and the impact of their work is both deep and lasting.

Teams are more in synch, are more able to navigate through difficult times, and are clearly focused on their common purpose. I'm excited that this book, *The Beauty of Conflict: Harnessing Your Team's Competitive Advantage*, is now available. It's a must read for anyone working in teams in any kind of organization. If you think that conflict is the problem, think again! Susan and CrisMarie's book will help turn the elephant in the room to your organization's competitive advantage."

Rachel Davey
The Haven Institute Executive Director

"We partnered with Thrive! during a crucial time in our growth. We applied the Thrive! team and communication tools to help us enhance the performance of our leadership team and improve our company culture, which contributed significantly to our success going public as one of the top five performing IPOs of 2016!"

Evan Fein
Impinj CFO

"I worked with Thrive! on two different teams: one I was a member of and one I led. Each time Thrive!'s work was game-changing for our business. Our ability to work productively with conflict real-time changed conflict into not a problem but a *resource* for creative and innovative problem solving. Our work with Thrive! helped transform not only my team but my entire organization. This book is a must read for anyone wanting to create organizational change."

Andrew Walker
Nationwide Bank President

"*The Beauty of Conflict* provides the practical model for becoming an influential leader, creating high-performing teams and transforming conflict into innovative results—no small undertaking! CrisMarie and Susan partnered with us to develop our leadership team, senior leaders, and managers. Their approach outlined in *The Beauty of Conflict* is practical, sound, and effective. I happily recommend them and the book!"

Amy Whaley
Marchex VP People Services

"As the GM of Trustworthy Computing at Microsoft I lead an organization full of subject matter experts. Working with CrisMarie Campbell and Susan Clarke gave me the methodology, tools, and guidance to transform not just my leadership team, but my whole organization, into a high-performing cohesive team! *Beauty of Conflict* should be required reading for every leader!"

Peter Cullen
Microsoft, Former GM Trustworthy Computing

"I partnered with Thrive! in the midst of a transition. They're now my trusted team advisors. Not only do CrisMarie and Susan clearly reflect back how they see me so I become a better leader, they work with my leadership team and entire organization, resulting in us increasing Wolfe's profit each year."

Terri Wolfe
Wolfe Mining, President

"How invigorating to see such a powerful body of work on conflict and communication. We engaged Thrive! at Seattle Children's Hospital when we were in a moment of crisis in a high-profile project. CrisMarie and Susan coached us through not only overcoming conflict, but learning to embrace and exploit it to our benefit.

At Children's, at UW Medicine, and now at Skagit, we adopted 'Check It Out' as a powerful tool to address intrapersonal disagreements. It became part of our communication vernacular, and as it did, we witnessed increases in team effectiveness and willingness to engage one another directly.

When team members independently recognized our ability to overcome the passive aggressive phenomenon known as 'Pacific Northwest Nice,' we out performed our original goals! I'm delighted to see these tools, stories, and cumulative experiences in this book for the benefit of all organizations—so they, too, can unleash the underestimated power of conflict!"

Patrick Dolan
Skagit Regional Health Senior Director of Application Services

"Conflict is never my favorite thing, and truth-telling can lead to conflict. But I've found that when we face this fact with integrity, an alchemical change turns coworkers into true creators. CrisMarie and Susan describe this process in *The Beauty of Conflict*, and I'd recommend this book to anyone who wants to improve team performance at work or anywhere else."

Martha Beck
Martha Beck Inc. CEO and Author

"Many leaders see conflict as a sign of an unhealthy team, but as *The Beauty of Conflict* pointedly shows, this is a huge mistake. Leaders who learn to leverage healthy conflict for the good of their team will forge a culture that thrives in the face of uncertainty. *The Beauty of Conflict* gives you the awareness and tools to help your team fight fair."

Todd Henry,
Author of The Accidental Creative

"Best leadership development program, ever! CrisMarie and Susan created and delivered our leadership development program at Clearwire over a decade ago. I've been to several other leadership development programs since and nothing's compared. I had to bring them in to Twitch when we wanted to develop the EQ of our leaders here. This book is a must read if you're a leader who wants to increase your influence."

Margi Lee-Johnson
Twitch, Director, Global People Operations

THE Beauty ~~PAIN~~ OF CONFLICT

HARNESSING YOUR TEAM'S COMPETITIVE ADVANTAGE

CRISMARIE CAMPBELL AND SUSAN CLARKE

Whitefish, Montana

THE BEAUTY OF CONFLICT
HARNESSING YOUR TEAM'S COMPETITIVE ADVANTAGE

Published by Two Hummingbird Press, Whitefish, Montana

We often tell stories to help you relate to the situations. The stories told are based on our actual client team experiences. Because most people don't want to reveal their oh, sh*t! moments, we have taken liberties with the actual names and industries, and we have changed some details. Every so often we have combined certain clients and their stories to give you a better learning example.

Quantity discounts are available on bulk purchases of this book for organizations. Special books or book excerpts can also be created to fit specific needs. For information, please contact Two Hummingbird Press, 704C E. 13th St. (124), Whitefish, MT 59937.

Cover and Interior Layout: Yvonne Parks, www.pearcreative.ca
Illustrations: Jack Davis, www.daviscreative.com
Indexer: Elena Gwynn, www.quillandinkindexing.com
Editor: Stacy Ennis, www.stacyennis.com

Library of Congress Control Number: 2017914765

Publisher's Cataloging-In-Publication Data
(Prepared by The Donohue Group, Inc.)

Names: Campbell, CrisMarie. | Clarke, Susan, 1960-
Title: The beauty of conflict : harnessing your team's competitive advantage / CrisMarie Campbell and Susan Clarke.
Other Titles: Pain of conflict
Description: Whitefish, Montana : Two Hummingbird Press, [2017] | Title also contains the word "pain" with a strikethrough. | Includes bibliographical references and index.
Identifiers: ISBN 9780999450109 | ISBN 9780999450116 (mobi) | ISBN 9780999450123 (ePub)
Subjects: LCSH: Conflict management. | Teams in the workplace. | Personnel management. | Creative ability in business.
Classification: LCC HD42 .C36 2017 (print) | LCC HD42 (ebook) | DDC 658.4/053--dc23

DEDICATION

This book is dedicated to Bennett Wong and Jock McKeen,
who founded The Haven.

They taught, and showed, us the power of relationship.

This wisdom fundamentally changed our relationship,
our lives, and how we do business.

TABLE OF CONTENTS

INTRODUCTION
What Makes Conflict Beautiful?

No one likes conflict. Not even us.

Most people weren't trained in it nor provided good models growing up.

Most people think conflict is painful and an impediment to work, so they make choices to avoid, manage, or defuse it by choosing to either overpower the situation to end and win an argument or go silent to keep the peace.

This seems like a good idea at an individual level. After all, who wants to experience the discomfort, other people's reactions, or the tension of conflict?

When leaders and teams avoid, manage, or defuse conflict, they wind up mired in politics, gossip, and back-channel maneuvering. Team meetings are boring as people defer to the leader or the loudest member. Team members are uninspired, or worse disengaged, and their performance is mediocre at best. Ultimately, turnover increases because no one wants to stay on the team that's so dysfunctional.

Sound familiar?

If it does, you are not alone. In a 2014 Gallup survey of employee engagement, only 31.5 percent of employees were *engaged* (psychologically committed and making positive contributions at work), 51 percent of employees were disengaged, and 17.5 percent were actively disengaged.[1] We believe there's a direct correlation between employee engagement and the degree to which people embrace and use conflict.

This is not another book with formulas for addressing conflict because it's a good team-management strategy. Rather, approached right, conflict is a *gift* that every member of your team can bring to the table. We say, "Use it! Don't defuse it!"

In this book, we provide you with simple, practical tools that you can apply with your team—or in any relationship—to make a positive impact using the natural energy of conflict to create innovative, profitable, and beautiful results. You'll get both big-picture concepts to help you get your team to look at conflict differently, and detailed tools for how to work with and through the tension that comes up when you and your team begin embracing conflict. Throughout this book, we will demonstrate the tools with plenty of real-life business examples from our 15+ years of working with Fortune 100 companies to start-ups, illustrating what works and what doesn't.

THE CHANGE

Imagine looking forward to your next team meeting. Imagine experiencing tension and conflict in the room and thinking, "This is going to lead to a great and innovative outcome—we just don't know what it is yet!"

When you as a leader strive to produce a cohesive and aligned team, embracing and using conflict will help you harness the team's potential by accessing creative breakthroughs, driving the team's competitive advantage.

Your team, rather than deferring to the leader's or loudest member's opinion, will come up with creative breakthroughs together. You'll arrive at ideas that none of you considered before walking into the room. Team momentum increases because people are inspired and engaged. No longer does one person have to pull the team along; they're pushing ahead together.

THE MODEL

We will walk you through our revolutionary approach to embracing conflict, our Path to Collective Creativity Team Performance Model. It takes you from your vision to that critical oh, sh*t! moment and choice point.

An oh, sh*t! moment is literally the *potential power source for creative solutions*. It is a rally cry for shared creativity, should you choose to listen and accept the call. Each one of these moments, if handled well, creates the possibility for an innovative, creative, and profitable result.

We'll uncover how teams have undermined team performance by habitually opting out of conflict, using their individual communication styles to manage, avoid, or defuse conflict. We'll introduce you to three key areas that are crucial for achieving extraordinary results by opting in and using conflict to make your team great: the ME, the WE, and the BUSINESS.

COLLECTIVE CREATIVITY PATH

3

We start with the ME because how you are with yourself in the midst of conflict is central for your capacity to be present and engage effectively during conflict.

Next, we focus on the WE because that's where conflict shows up.

Once the ME and the WE are aligned, we focus on the BUSINESS.

In our work with hundreds of leaders and their teams, we have run, walked, and stumbled through this path from oh, sh*t! to collective creativity many, many times. We will give you the concepts, tools, and tips to turn around your team in an instant when you get stuck and how to reap the rewards to come up with an innovative business solution to your toughest problems. We will also give you key business tools to maintain the positive results going forward on your team.

USING THIS BOOK

We patterned this book after the books we enjoy reading, such as *All I Really Need to Know I Learned in Kindergarten* and *Rework*. We've provided you with short pieces that you can read quickly and get a practical tip, nugget of inspiration, or to provide you with a new way of thinking.

We will tell stories to help you relate to the situations, stories based on the team experiences of our clients. While the stories are true, we have taken liberties with the actual names and industries, and we have combined details and client characteristics to better illustrate the learning principles.

We've outlined our approach to conflict in six sections that follow our Path to Collective Creativity Team Performance Model. You can read the sections in order or just open the book to any old section, read it, and walk away with an insight that will help you create a more successful team!

WHY READ THIS BOOK?

The power of people working together, aka: teamwork, is our greatest unlimited and, frankly, wildly untapped potential. However, until we fully recognize that conflict is the energetic engine for transformation, innovation, and creativity, we won't opt in! Conflict is NOT comfortable, nor does any sane person go looking for conflict.

Any time people gather, conflict naturally emerges because no two people are alike. Therein lies the potential: When we embrace and engage with our different points of view, our oh, sh*t! moments take us not to *right* or *wrong*, but to *places no one has gone before*! Conflict is the source of amazing transformation.

Read on to learn how you can turn your source of pain into a source of creativity on your team! Won't that be beautiful?

Engage!

ABOUT THE AUTHORS

We are CrisMarie Campbell and Susan Clarke, life and business partners who have been coaching from the center of conflict for more than fifteen years. While we work, live, and even write together (this book, for example), we are also different people with unique reasons why we embrace conflict as central to our lives. Throughout the book, we will write from a cohesive *we*, but we will also tell you our personal individual stories. But before we go any further, we want to offer some insight into who we each are and why we chose to build our lives around using conflict in relationships and teams.

CrisMarie Campbell

I'll be honest, I hate conflict! I have been a professional conflict avoider most of my life. My definition of a good relationship used to be one where everything was smooth.

My father was an Army colonel. Every night at the dinner table I ran the gauntlet hoping he wouldn't get upset. Bad things happened when Dad was mad. Each evening at dinner, my mom, brother, sister, and I knew he would ask us, "How was school today?"

He expected a status report outlining all our achievements. My older sister's mission was to buck the system. Her answer was often an insolent, "Fine!" This ignited the flame of anger in The Colonel.

Yikes! I was so afraid of his reaction, I took it upon myself to jump in the middle of the fray to put out the fire. Some nights, I'd offer a rephrase: "I think what she meant to say is...." Other nights, I'd distract my dad by focusing on something good: "I got an A on my math test!" Or I'd ask a question to change the subject: "Dad, what chores do we need to get done this weekend?"

Defusing conflict became my superpower. When I got older, I was even better at defusing conflict. By adulthood, I could pull a group of people together to keep the peace and accomplish amazing things. It led me to my passion—teamwork, which really came to light in sports. I wasn't an athlete in high school, but I took up rowing at the University of Washington in Seattle. I was team captain and stroke (the leadership role in the boat) for the 1985 National Championship Team.

I went on to compete at the elite level and made the USA 1987 National and 1988 Olympic teams. The difference between those two boats was night and day, and I learned the importance of teamwork.

In 1987, the Russians had been dominant players for years, and none of the competing teams were expected to do well against them. When our USA team arrived at the World Championships in Denmark, we were ranked lowest and put in the outside lane. Water in the outside lane was choppy water, a deterrent to speed in rowing. The Russians were on the other side of the course in protected, smooth water. Halfway through the race our coxswain called out, "We are moving on the Russians!" I was shocked, and I could feel the energy swell in the boat as we surged with power and grace. I remember the sound of our oarlocks and the splash of our blades hitting the water in sync. We cut through the water like a hot knife in butter, moving through the Russians until they were behind us.

In the end, Romania won gold, and our USA team won silver. Even though my team didn't come in first, we were all ecstatic to have toppled the mighty Russians. A large, blonde Romanian woman picked me and another US teammate up in celebration.

In 1987, we were a team that was connected and aligned. I was slated to be the stroke but was young and inexperienced. I gladly moved to the other end of the boat, the bow position, so a more experienced stroke could lead us. We all trusted each other, we got through conflicts well, and we bore general goodwill.

In the 1988 Olympics, we were expected to medal, but instead we came in at a disappointing sixth. It wasn't because our athletes were weak. Both the 1987 National and 1988 Olympic boats had high-caliber rowers. The problem wasn't skill; it was lack of teamwork. That year, we had factions and egos. One gal seemed to be in it for herself, fascinated with making it on TV. As for me, I had been injured but had passed the tests to make the boat. When the last-minute decision was made to use an experimental boat, I remained silent, even though I didn't like the idea. I just felt lucky to be on the team, so I didn't speak up. Later, after our loss, the boat we used was scrapped due to a defective design. This poor result was the first clue that my childhood strategy of not speaking up wasn't working.

The difference between those two teams was palpable. In 1987, one plus one equaled eleven; in 1988, one plus one equaled minus one. It was then when I learned the difference between a championship team (1987) and a boat full of champions (1988).

After the games I went on to work at Boeing as a mechanical engineer and was assigned to a test project for the design of the 777, a major redesign of the 757. We were a cross-functional team representing the complete design functions, manufacturing, technology, operations, and more. At the time, computer-aided design (CAD) was new.

Since its early days, Boeing designed and built airplanes by first creating a life-size physical mock-up of the plane in cheaper materials. If there was a design problem, we engineers would go to the mock-up together and figure out a new solution.

On this project our cross-functional team, which trusted each other, had a risky but innovative idea. We suggested to the leadership at Boeing that we scrap the physical mock-up and do the entire design on the computer.

That decision was controversial, because Boeing is risk-averse as a culture; yet they agreed to support us.

Throughout the project, our computer-only process delivered. We had fewer design issues, and it revolutionized how Boeing now builds airplanes. This was a powerful lesson for me about what great teams can produce in business. It was another lesson for me in the power of teamwork.

Despite my positive experience at Boeing, I was a misplaced people-person who wound up in engineering. I went back to school for my MBA and got a job at Arthur Andersen. I was the on-site manager for a team of six on a project for a software client. The senior manager from Arthur Andersen stopped by to give us the project strategy plan. I listened and thought, *this is not going to solve the client's problem*. Rather than say what I knew, I *asked*, "Do you think this is going to solve the client's problem?"

The manager's face tightened. "Of course it is," he replied. "Get to work!" I was catapulted back in time to my dad's dinner table. I shut up and followed the plan.

At the end of six months, the partners at Arthur Andersen wanted more work with this prestigious client, so they brought in the client VP for a conversation. Here we were: my three bosses, Arthur Andersen partners, the client VP, my senior manager, and myself. I sat along the wall, while the others all sat around the table.

The partners asked the client, "Tell us, how can we help you more?"

The VP turned and pointed to me. "Well, you know that project CrisMarie led? That was a disaster. A complete disaster."

That was one of my career oh, sh*t! moments, and a clue that my childhood strategy wasn't working.

I knew then and there that I wanted the courage to speak up and be brave and bold so nothing like that would happen again. It turned out that my *superpower* had serious limitations.

Shortly thereafter, I met Susan who worked with conflict very differently. She was helping groups transform into teams by dealing with their differences creatively. The innovative solutions that emerged on those teams were phenomenal. Plus, Susan herself was so alive. I wanted what she had. We officially joined forces professionally in 2002, and I've been in conflict ever since—in a great way!

Susan Clarke

At the age of twenty-four, I was diagnosed with non-Hodgkin lymphoma. Immediately, I began fighting the good fight against cancer. I became fully engaged in being positive and doing whatever was needed to handle an aggressive treatment protocol. Nine months in, I finished my cancer treatment scorecard of testing, and I felt confident that I would beat cancer and get on with my life.

You can imagine my surprise when I walked into my doctor's office and got my grade: F.

Now, of course, that is not how she delivered the news. In fact, her words landed harder, "The treatments aren't working."

"The cancer is advancing."

"We don't have another option."

"You probably have six months to live."

"You might want to get your affairs in order."

Oh, sh*t! I thought. How did I get here? And, what the hell do I do now? I was stunned into silence. I mumbled under my breath and left.

That was a turning point in my life. There was no Hail Mary pass that would get me out of this game alive.

On my way out, I saw a flyer: *Life, Death and Transition*. Without really thinking, I took a copy and walked out of the office. Once outside, I looked at the flyer. It was by a woman named Elisabeth Kubler-Ross, and I had no idea who she was. Life, death, and transition were not subject matters to which I had given much thought. Heck, I was only twenty-four years old.

Still, I needed help. So I wrote to her:

> *Elisabeth,*
>
> *Apparently I'm dying and fairly soon. I don't really know how to deal with that. I don't have any money. I have no real clue who you are. But I picked up your flyer and wanted to see if there was any chance that I could come to your workshop.*
>
> *Thanks for considering,*
> *Susie*

I added my phone number to the bottom and stuck that little note in the mail. (Yes, this was long before email.)

That was my first conscious experience of opting in and facing an oh, sh*t! moment. I dove in head first. I could have opted out, gotten angry, and found someone to blame. I could have given up. Or, I could have taken the path of least resistance and continued to live my little life the same way I always had and let the cancer take me.

I chose something different. Writing that letter was my first step toward a better journey that gained positive momentum.

She said, "Come."

I attended Kubler-Ross's workshop, during which she presented me with a challenge. "You and I are not really that different," she said. "Someone just told you when you were going to die. Now you are focusing on dying or not dying, and that is not living!"

Living, I learned, is turning toward whatever life presents and diving into it. It's being curious. It's not about fighting cancer, rather, it's about engaging in life. It's facing whatever there is to face, throwing myself into the mess and swimming my way through it.

Kubler-Ross launched me on a path that helped me discover the guiding motto of my life: *Choose to live. Choose to be curious. Fearlessly or fearfully face whatever is in front of you. Do not step away from chaos, conflict, and uncertainty. Instead, step in and reap the magic and the miracles.*

My life journey didn't end in six months, and for that I am eternally grateful. But I won't lie, it wasn't easy.

The next step landed me at The Haven Institute, a personal and professional development center in British Columbia, Canada, in a program called *Come Alive*. The Haven offered a different path, which was to consider that my tumors had stories from my past that needed to be told and felt. As I followed that path, I also engaged other alternative healing methods. My doctors thought I was nuts, yet I got healthier.

The tricky part was, I still needed the doctors on my team along *with* the alternative healers and psychologists. My vision was to be healthy again. I needed these smart, opinionated people to work together on *Project Susan*. I had to face my crazy past, the questions, and the chaos of doing a little bit of everything while throwing myself into that conflict in conjunction with staying curious.

It was extremely difficult and humbling to discover just how stubborn, defensive, and resistant I could be. But I kept coming back to that choice point: Am I in? Or, am I out? Choose!

I learned to listen. I learned to speak up. I learned the incredible value in differences and the possibility that comes from making space for the new and different. I also learned about the miracles created when people who have different points of view collaborate on a common problem they both care deeply about and want a successful outcome.

My experience at The Haven was a foundation on which I could challenge myself to keep opting in, even when it was not life or death. This book is about how to opt in, not because you are dying, but because it awakens your creativity!

Now, years later, I apply that learning to the challenges facing leaders every day. My work with my partner, CrisMarie, revolves around helping leaders, teams, and organizations face and embrace their *Oh, sh*t! How did we get here?* moments.

Leaders need this kind of guidance today more than ever. We could all stand to step up our games and quit fighting and blaming each other.

Opt in. It may get messy, but if you stay curious and interested in all the possibilities, especially the ones far afield from your own, I do believe you will discover something totally new and magical.

SECTION ONE
Oh, Sh*t!

SECTION ONE
OVERVIEW

When we bring together intelligent, passionate people to share a big vision, our tendency is to think, *This will be awesome! We're going to change the world.*

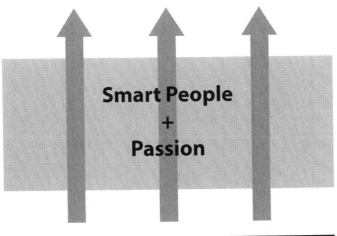

WHAT WE EXPECT

Change the World

Smart People
+
Passion

Goal or Vision

But that doesn't always happen.

More often, all those smart people have different opinions—and they all think they're right. Tension builds and people grapple for control and get caught in the power struggle of the right-wrong trap. The result? Even more tension and ambiguity.

This lands us smack dab into an oh, sh*t! moment.

WHAT REALLY HAPPENS

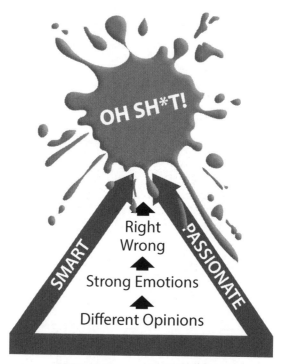

GOAL or VISION

There is good news, though. This oh, sh*t! moment is the source of a team's potential creative energy.

The bad news is that it's called an oh, sh*t! moment for a reason: conflict feels uncomfortable. We feel incapable of responding to the situation. This is a critical choice point for leaders and teams. It's the crossroads between, *Do I play it safe and opt out,* and *do I opt in to create something innovative and transformational?*

What if your team doesn't experience these moments of tension and discomfort? If your group always gets along, it's time for a wake-up call. You are in the business of making things happen, and *that* requires some juice.

You *want* to run into oh, sh*t! moments. You *need* to run into oh, sh*t! moments!

In this section, we'll discuss why teams fail and get into the gory details of some of our client's oh, sh*t! moments. As we've said, don't worry, the identifying details have been changed to keep our client's situations private.

Our goal is to normalize the oh, sh*t! moment because, for humans working with other humans, it is bound to happen. How you handle those moments will make or break your team's short- and long-term success. We aim to help you and your team be consistently successful. Read on!

CHAPTER 1
Why Teams Fail—It's Not What You Think

It's not lack of talent that causes team mediocrity. It's *lack of conflict.*

The prevailing perception is that *good* teams shy away from conflict. Doing so makes them look efficient or kind. The truth is, they are holding back from experiencing precious moments. Yes, *precious moments.* They're missing opportunities for collective creativity.

We refer to these tension points as oh, sh*t! moments. Maybe you don't use such language. But have you ever noticed that even if you don't say it aloud, inside your head you sometimes hear a booming, *Oh, sh*t! How did I get here?*

That's the inner experience of being smack-dab in the middle of tension and ambiguity without any immediate answers or solutions to get past the discomfort.

Imagine you're the head of a manufacturing company. In a team meeting, your leadership team is discussing the last steps in production for your awesome new change-the-world product. Tom, head of operations, says, "We aren't going to be able to produce the number we targeted. We didn't get the shipment of wafers for the box."

You say (whether out loud or to yourself), "Oh, sh*t!" What happens next is a bit of a free-for-all.

Out loud you say, "Who's responsible for this? Why didn't we know earlier?"

The CFO barks out, "Look, my team did their part. Get it together, Tom."

Head of sales jumps in, "Damn it, my sales team worked their asses off, and now this happens. They're going to look like fools to the customers!"

Too often, the blame and banter points to a scapegoat and delays solving the problem. Another common scenario is that team members stay quiet, scatter, and then work harder on their own areas, which leaves the problem and frustration unaddressed.

WHAT CAUSES OH, SH*T! MOMENTS?

We most commonly experience oh, sh*t! moments through efforts of relating to each other and working well together. We want productivity, connection, and collaboration. The path to that end is littered with overwhelming points caused by the gaps and tension between us.

These moments are natural. Teams typically begin the collaborative process inspired and excited about the possibility of working together and successfully accomplishing a shared vision—a better world, a great gadget, an awesome book! And naturally, the end result, gadget or book will turn out better if the process has more than one perspective or genius creating it. Two, three, four, or more people are almost always better than one, especially if they all agree it's a great vision!

Each is inspired. Each is unique.

Each person contributes his or her distinct piece to this collective journey. It's no different on your team, whether you are a leader or a member.

You may like your teammates and even love their brands of genius, but at some point you will clash. You will think Kate is crazy because she wants more detail or color. You will want results faster than William, who believes increased speed causes quality to suffer. You try to talk both of them out of their positions and persuade them to move on. Kate will dig in her heels. William will refuse to listen. In response, you either bully your way through or silently suffer, both of which are increasingly uncomfortable because you actually like your teammates. You like your shared vision. You like how your team plans, but it's not working!

Avoidance, whether through being a bully or keeping quiet, doesn't work. That little inner voice just gets louder: *Oh, sh*t! Oh, sh*t! OH, SH*T!*

Let's say that instead of using your habitual *coping* options, you stop. You listen. You say to your teammates, "Wait. I'm uncomfortable, nervous, and uncertain. We're at odds with each other, and I don't know how to fix it!" You might even express your worry that they will abandon the project altogether.

That's not usually how it goes in business and on teams. People don't like to admit discomfort, uncertainty or fear. Leaders, especially, tend to think that admitting these truths out loud shows weakness. They worry they'll lose their team's respect. Most businesspeople won't even acknowledge their vulnerability even to themselves. But as coaches, we have seen that such statements of vulnerability and truth are precisely what lie beneath the surface, even if everything looks good from the outside.

Here's the root of the problem: people want to be independent and autonomous while also wanting to be relational and collaborative. These are inherently opposing and essential drivers of being human, and they create tremendous tension. It puts us at odds with ourselves and with others, especially within organizations, teams, and significant relationships!

Oh, sh*t! is where you—including the way you see the world, your preferences, approach, style, all of what we call your *self definition*—meet others on your team. It's both a big black hole and an amazing opportunity. You must engage that potential to make a quantum leap to collective brilliance. Ask yourself: would you rather settle for mediocrity or risk the discomfort of stepping up to the very edge of a black hole to access the potential of your team?

An oh, sh*t! moment is literally the *potential power source for creative solutions*. It is a rally cry for shared creativity should you choose to listen and accept the call. Each one of these instances, if handled well, creates the possibility for an innovative, creative, and profitable result.

In our work with hundreds of leaders and their teams, we have run, walked, and stumbled through this path from oh, sh*t! to collective creativity many, many times. Through hard work and vulnerability, these individuals and groups have accessed collaborative genius. We'll share some of the simple and practical tools we use with our clients so you, too, can access the tremendous potential energy of an oh, sh*t! moment to drive greater alignment, productivity, creativity, and innovation.

CHAPTER 2
Oh, Sh*t! We're Not in Kansas Anymore (and Other Stories)

Several years back, we facilitated a university leadership team in the midst of a breakdown.

"Okay, you asked for it. I'm angry and I think this is a waste of time!" yelled Eric, one of the executives. He slammed his fist on the table. "People are saying a lot about how I haven't done my job, but no one says any of it to me in person. Why should I trust these people?"

Interminable silence followed. This was a critical moment in the success or failure of the meeting and the team itself. As the management consultants and facilitators, we needed to ensure the growth opportunity did not slip by.

Eric was a senior member of the team, responsible for a critical project that had failed. We didn't like that Eric was yelling and pounding the table. But he'd said something real, raw, and honest. For the better part of the morning, the team had tiptoed in a brittle, artificial harmony that, frankly, was unproductive.

Susan spoke up. "Eric, I get that you're angry," she said. "Even though

I'm uncomfortable with the volume and your fist hitting the table, I'm glad you spoke honestly."

Eric looked at Susan, weighing his response. Finally, he said, "I think I have the most to lose here. Why should I be interested in trying to fix the damage done? Apparently, it has been my lack of leadership and mismanagement that has resulted in most of our current issues. People around this table basically think I'm stupid." His voice was still strong, but there was a definite shift in tone.

"Look, Eric," Susan replied, "if you were really going to lose your job over this, do you think you would have a seat at the table today? I doubt people think you're stupid. They may have some concerns about how you've been doing your job. If you really want a straight answer on that, now is the time to ask for it."

This university leadership team had been ignoring their interpersonal issues for a long time. Their efforts to have appropriate and respectful meetings had resulted in mounds of underground tension, which made forward progress almost impossible.

Again, the ensuing silence was big. But with our support, Eric courageously stepped back into the mess and asked for some honest, open feedback.

What followed were straight, real comments about things Eric had done to cause the failure of a key project and undermine the leadership team's success. Absolutely no one, however, thought Eric was stupid. People were upset and angry about what Eric was avoiding and how he had approached the project.

The tricky part was that none of his team members knew how, or even felt it was okay, to speak up about such uncomfortable, negative judgments. With this lack of empowerment, the concerns all went underground. Everyone knew there were issues, and Eric definitely knew people were upset, but none of it had been discussed.

After the team unloaded their direct, clear, and hard feedback, Eric wanted a breather. He exited the room alone, and we all took a break. Ten minutes later, he returned and we resumed. He acknowledged that hearing the honest opinions and having a chance to process and integrate what he had heard was enough to bring him back to the table.

Eric ultimately agreed with all of the interpretations. He shared that he felt overwhelmed with the demands of his position and, at the risk of appearing incompetent, had been uncomfortable asking for help. Instead he had tried to do everything on his own and had indeed let a few highly critical issues slip. As a result, the project had failed.

While everything was not fixed then and there, the dynamics of the team became remarkably different. The team committed to engaging in conflict, even if it might get messy and *disrespectful*. They created a new, innovative plan to recover from the failed project. They each agreed that going forward they would speak up when they saw unproductive behaviors in each other.

In a follow-up session, we helped the team more effectively rebuild its cohesion and the organization's success. Today, they are aligned and creative because they thrive on healthy conflict, even when it isn't comfortable.

OH, SH*T! WE'RE NOT ALIGNED

For six months, we worked with the leadership team of a software business unit within a larger international computer company, which we'll call MCW. The business unit had a key role in influencing the rest of the computer company to improve their products' experience. The team was finally ready to roll out their organizational direction, including their purpose and goals, to the rest of the organization. We would facilitate the company-wide meeting by conducting team-building and sharing the leadership team's process to reach organizational clarity. The day before the meeting, we had a coaching call with Todd, the president. The next day, his leadership team would communicate the new business clarity to all employees and receive initial feedback. We had last met with the entire team a month earlier.

"We are all set for tomorrow," Todd said, his voice strong and confident. "The entire organization will be here. We've put together talking points for the business clarity we've been working on since the last off-site meeting."

"We'd planned to bring your leadership team back together for a quick review prior to the rollout," CrisMarie replied. "There were some questions about the business clarity direction when we were with you last. Did you work out those issues?"

"We are good to go," Todd affirmed.

CrisMarie pushed to make sure. "Are you sure about this, Todd? You can't leave this to chance. The team has got to be rock solid and aligned when you present tomorrow. We can get on a last-minute Skype call with the team to make sure."

"No need. Yes, I'm sure." Todd sounded confident, and we moved forward.

The next day nearly fifty people filled the room, sitting at round tables with their own teams. Each leadership team member sat with their direct reports. We introduced the Path to Collective Creativity team model. Afterward, Todd spoke to the high-level business clarity.

"This is our core purpose: to change the DNA of MCW so that it delivers great experiences! Before I go any further, is that a surprise to anyone?" Todd paused for comments.

"Well, actually, I don't think that is what our core purpose is," someone said. We swiveled our heads searching the crowd for the source of the comment. We were surprised to see it was Steve, one of the leaders sitting with his team, who had spoken up. Steve is an introvert. During our off-site the previous month, Steve stayed quiet, saying he needed time to process before he could commit.

Oh, sh*t! From the onset of working with this team, our biggest concern had been that the group would finalize the clarity piece without everyone buying in. In this moment, our fear was justified! Steve had finally processed his thoughts and now disagreed with Todd.

The all-employee organizational event quickly shifted from rolling out the business clarity to debating and redefining clarity in front of the entire organization. This is not an ideal scenario to showcase a leadership team's cohesion. A great debate ensued, and in the end another leadership team member agreed with Steve. Oh, great! A few brave folks spoke up and directly called into question the cohesion of the leadership team. We wanted people to have a chance to respond so we let it go on for a bit, but we knew how to transform messy into real and recover.

CrisMarie interrupted the process and took a bullet. She acknowledged our part in the mess and reflected back what she was hearing from folks. She knew, though, the game-changing comment really needed to come from the leader. She turned to Todd urging him to model what we had been coaching him and the team on for the last six months.

Todd rose to the occasion. "Look, I take responsibility for this," he began. "I thought we were aligned and committed, but I clearly didn't go back and make sure everyone had shared their concerns. I may have assumed folks who disagreed would've spoken up earlier. That was my mistake. So now that we are here, let me roll out a couple more related organizational clarity items. The leadership team will have some more discussions at our round tables and finalize the core purpose and other business clarity items—again."

We debriefed the previous day's events the next day with the leadership team. They finally hammered out the business clarity pieces, getting full, explicit buy-in and commitment. The team walked away stronger for it and rolled out the business clarity to the organization shortly thereafter at another organization-wide meeting, underscoring their learning from the experience.

Later, Todd told us that first meeting was one of the worst days for him in his tenure as president. But instead of wallowing in regret, Todd made his oh, sh*t! moment work for him. It was key learning for him and the leadership team about the importance of full, explicit commitment. When they finally successfully rolled out the business clarity, they acknowledged the importance of getting commitment and the inevitable chaos that would ensue if they didn't.

This was a hard, but important, lesson. It resulted in greater cohesion and business clarity. While no one on the team would want to repeat the chaotic day, they are better for it. Now, when they meet before any key organization-wide communications, they ensure a full, explicit commitment. We'll talk about what that involves later in the book.

In both of these examples, the university leadership team and software business unit leadership team were each faced with more conflict than they had the capacity to process. These moments were neither pretty nor comfortable, but each time at least one person was willing to show up vulnerable and curious, and that shifted the situation. Those who spoke up influenced the rest of the team, and that evoked creativity to resolve the business issue. Every oh, sh*t! moment is a potential source of creativity and innovation, but only if you opt in. Unfortunately, that's not what usually happens.

What usually happens is that people want to run like hell to get away from an oh, sh*t! moment. Let's take a look at how most people handle oh, sh*t! moments. Maybe you can relate.

SECTION TWO
Opting Out

SECTION TWO
OVERVIEW

People often have low tolerance for tension and ambiguity. Conflict causes tension, both within ourselves and with others. It generates ambiguity about a person or team's focus and makes us feel out of control. So, rather than tolerate conflict, people cope by trying to defuse the tension. They attempt to control the conflict in the best way they know: by avoiding it. We call this opting out.

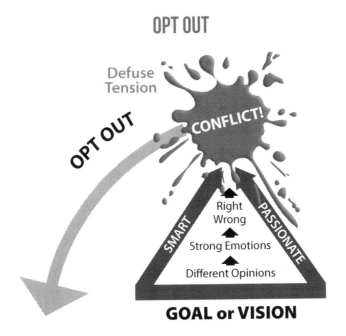

OPT OUT

Defuse Tension

OPT OUT

CONFLICT!

SMART

PASSIONATE

Right
Wrong

Strong Emotions

Different Opinions

GOAL or VISION

Avoiding conflict seems like a good idea at an individual level. After all, who wants to experience the discomfort, other people's reactions, or the tension of conflict? But avoiding conflict is detrimental to a team because it stalls team creativity.

In this section, we'll go into detail about opting out. While people find many ways to opt out, the three most typical styles are as Superstar, Accommodator, and Separator. We'll show you why each time you make the choice to opt out and avoid oh, sh*t! moments, you undermine, eliminate, and defuse the potential energy that drives team creativity. Even though you feel better in the short-term because the tension and ambiguity are gone, the result is that creative energy also escapes, like air out of a balloon.

If you've been opting out, the likelihood is you'll keep opting out. Heck, you're human! The key, however, is to recognize when you are making that choice and notice the impact so you can make a different decision when you want to or are ready to. We'll show you how to recognize, notice, and decide to opt-in to conflict in this section.

Let's start with a story that shows the huge bottom-line cost when teams opt out.

CHAPTER 3
How Opting Out Cost $750,000!

We worked with a telecom company that had bumped into an oh, sh*t! moment nine months earlier and had opted out ever since. They had hired two other consulting firms before asking us to help them on their *network tower* strategy. Both previous attempts to roll out the strategy had failed. They wanted our help to develop a new network tower strategy that would work.

We said we would work with the team if they agreed to first spend the morning fostering healthy conflict before we got to their strategy. Shortly into the first day, the tension between two vice presidents surfaced. Floyd, a member of the team looked at Ed, the EVP of networks and team leader, and said, "I don't know what we're doing here. This is a complete waste of time!" Then he turned to Luke, his teammate sitting on the other end of the table, leaned forward, pointed his finger and said, "I don't like you or trust you!"

We were stunned into a bit of silence. Susan recovered first and said, "Okay Floyd." Then she turned to Luke and asked him, "So what do you think?" Luke folded his arms, turned away, and said, "Ditto."

We dove in to discover what had broken down. Nine months earlier

Luke's department had been late handing off a deliverable to Floyd's team. In Floyd's view, Luke had not taken any responsibility when the entire project was late. Luke was angry because Floyd had been continuously undermining their department and didn't know why. Their two departments had been at war ever since.

Everyone else on the team knew about this issue, but no one dealt directly with the problem. It was clear that when the oh, sh*t! moment happened nine months earlier, they had opted out and had continued opting out ever since. As a result, resentment built, trust broke down, work stalled, and money flowed down the drain. The team kept trying to fix a process that wasn't broken rather than deal with the unresolved issues—until we showed up.

When it was clear the issue originated between Floyd and Luke, we spent thirty minutes debriefing the earlier incident. First, we introduced the VPs and the entire team to the value of vulnerability and curiosity. Then we mapped out our core communication tool, *Check It Out*, a powerful way to bridge differences.

Ed, the team leader, was first to show up real and vulnerable. He said, "I want to acknowledge that I let this go on for too long. I worked independently with you both, but I never really forced the issue at our team meetings. I want this resolved, because I know it's hindering our progress, and no one is happy."

It didn't take long for Floyd and Luke to show up real too. They each were willing to acknowledge their responsibility in creating the original oh, sh*t! moment.

Was it completely resolved in that meeting? No.

Did they learn some skills to continue to work through it? Yes.

At the end of the two days, the team agreed to go back to their original network tower strategy. The VPs and the entire team also committed to work through their unresolved issues during our six-month engagement. It gets better! During those six months, they rolled their strategy out without a hitch!

Still, that company lost a substantial amount of money throughout those previous nine months. They did an analysis, combining team member salaries, stalled progress on projects, and consulting fees for two other firms, and it was estimated that avoiding their oh, sh*t! moment cost the company more than $750,000.

Seems obvious to us, but it's your choice: Thirty minutes to clear up the conflict? Or, $750,000?

SIGNS OF TEAM CONFLICT

Most people don't recognize the signs of a team in conflict. They tend to think conflict is present only when team members are yelling at each other. We work with those situations too. But, more often, the signs of conflict show up in other, more subtle ways, with avoidance at the core. Team members may be:

- Bored at their meetings. Rather than having engaged, passionate, healthy, conflict and debate, they just give status reports, and the leader makes all the decisions.

- Managing their behavior in meetings but gossiping behind the scenes. They maintain the illusion of harmony, rather than being real and unfiltered in what they say. This leads to unproductive gossip and politics outside the meeting room walls.

- Doing their own thing by checking email during meetings, or otherwise disengaging from team activities. They focus on their own responsibilities rather than feeling committed to, and inspired by, collective results.

Team leaders may try to manage team dynamics through one-on-one team member conversations. Or even worse, like the team above, they create work-around processes so people don't have to work together. Not only is this exhausting, it rarely resolves the issue until the two people talk directly.

These are just some of the signs of unhealthy and unused team conflict. These behaviors waste time and money. Because they don't address and resolve the real issues, or use resources effectively, individual efforts are slowed, and there is no collective effort to move the business forward.

Alternatively, when they opt into conflict, they benefit from the juice of creativity and get to innovative results sooner. This impacts the bottom line in a healthy way.

If your team doesn't know how to navigate oh, sh*t! moments, opting out seems easy. That's what Floyd, Luke, and their entire team did. It's no wonder this is a typical response. Growing up, we weren't taught conflict resolution in school, and many of us never even learned to deal with conflict within our own families.

If you don't know how to handle moments of intense conflict at work, it's natural to resort to what you know and can control. In a team setting, that's typically your own area of work. You'll go to the meetings because you have to. You'll play nice with others until you can get back to your desk and do your *real* work. Sound familiar?

Stop it! That behavior sabotages the success of you, your team, and the business.

Remember: tension is your friend. Tension prods you to find new answers to old problems.

At the telecom company, a team of smart, capable people chose to opt out, which cost the company three-quarters of a million dollars. When they recognized signs of team conflict and chose to develop their level of candor, they were better able to deal with tough issues, and their collective results skyrocketed.

It is easy and seductive to avoid dealing with differences, to tell yourself that it is no big deal or it's not your problem. But the truth is that when you opt-out and don't deal with the conflict, you undermine your own success, the team's cohesion, and the business's bottom line. Just ask Ed.

Next, we'll show you the three styles people typically use to avoid, defuse, and opt-out of conflict. Which style do you use?

CHAPTER 4
Are You Undermining Team Success?

Teams that regularly produce creative and innovative solutions do not rely on the talents of one person. Rather, they have the capacity to hang in when the tension and ambiguity between team members rise to uncomfortable levels. They don't fall back on habitual coping mechanisms. Instead, they remain aware of themselves and others, and they continue to communicate openly through conflict to access innovative business solutions.

Teams that opt out during these tension-filled, ambiguous moments let all the air out of the creative balloon. They opt out in the name of efficiency, harmony, or personal comfort at the unintentional cost of effective, creative teamwork.

When you feel pressure and uncertainty, you must make a critical choice: opt in or opt out. People often choose to defuse tension through their automatic and habitual reactions. This helps them feel more in control, yet diminishes team creativity. We call these different habitual reactions *opt-out styles*. You'll feel empowered when you begin to notice the opt-out patterns of yourself and of others. You may be surprised how often you choose to defuse tension while believing you are helping the team, when in reality, you are optimizing your own comfort. To find out how you tend to opt out, take our online assessment at www.Thriveinc.com/beautyofconflict/bonus.

OPT-OUT STYLES

People find myriad ways to defuse tension and ambiguity and gain the illusion of control. We have found three of those opt-out styles to be most common: Superstar, Accommodator, and Separator. Which opt-out style do you most relate to? Which one is your favorite? Do you notice people on your team who fit into these styles? Let's look at each in detail.

Superstar

Superstars often feel impatient at work, especially in meetings. They think, "I know what we need to do. I'll never get them to agree. I'll just do it myself, and they'll thank me later."

This opt-out style involves a high focus on self, what we call *the ME*. If this is you, it means that when there is tension, you believe action will relieve the pressure. You feel an internal sense of urgency. You believe you already know the right answer or a good enough answer, and that getting everyone on board is an unnecessary waste of time.

Superstars are so focused on their own perspective that they can, and often do, ignore, dismiss, or even bully others. Sometimes this behavior is so unconscious that as a Superstar, you actually believe you're doing what is best and most efficient, and that people will thank you in the end for making it all happen.

Superstar key attributes:

- Need: Action and results
- Focus: On the ME—what I think, feel, and want
- Point of view: I'll speak up about my opinion, but I'm not so curious about others' opinions (takes too much time!)
- Verbal: Dominant in tone and speech
- Behavior: Do it myself for the good of the team

Observable signs of a Superstar:

- Actively moves the meeting along
- Appears impatient, paces, taps the desk, and interrupts
- Focused on moving the task forward
- Doing what you think is best, even though the team has not agreed on a path forward
- Dismissive or unaware of other people's reservations about going forward

Superstar blind spots:

Superstars are often unaware that they have left the other team members behind. As a result, they don't leverage the team's ideas or IQ. People with this opt-out style decide what is right for the team without checking in to see if people are on board or have other good ideas. The result is a suboptimal solution, limited buy-in, and usually tough implementation.

Leadership takeaway:

If you have this opt-out style, you tend to miss developing the skills and leadership abilities of the team, and that leaves you to carry the load. Your growth, and the team results, will improve when you notice your sense of urgency to do it yourself. Then, rather than acting on it, you can run your decision by the team or by someone who knows your tendency, to see if you're in your blind spot.

Accommodator

In a meeting with conflict, an Accommodator is often uncomfortable and thinking, "This is not okay. I've just got to get these two people to agree on something."

You might interject with something like, "I think what she meant to say is…" or smooth tension with, "I don't think we need to get upset about this."

An individual with this opt-out style has a high focus on others, or 'the WE.' If this is you, in the midst of tension, you focus on what others are saying, doing, wanting, and feeling. In fact, you probably do this so much that you stop being aware of what *you* think, feel, and want, and don't bring your own opinion forward.

In your discomfort with disagreements, raised voices, or signs of aggressive behavior, you as an Accommodator believe that helping others get along will relieve the tension. You work to reduce tension or upset by facilitating the discussion in meetings or approaching each person individually and managing conflict with one-on-one conversations.

The Accommodator's intense fear of conflict is the basis of this belief. You tend to think that teams and relationships are *good* only when everyone gets along and everything is smooth. Because of this, you focus on minimizing tension and disruptions. You come across as a peacekeeper by asking questions, facilitating the discussion, and rarely adding your own point of view.

As an Accommodator you tend to ignore yourself and can be quite out of touch with your own inner world. While you are gifted at reading the signs and cues from others, you miss yourself; meaning your opinion, gifts, feelings, and intention. You leave this out of the interaction as you busily help rebuild bridges between others.

Accommodator key attributes:

- Need: Peace and harmony
- Focus: On the WE, I just want people to get along
- Point of view: I don't reveal my opinion, but I am curious about other's opinions
- Verbal: Asking questions, conciliatory, and repeating back
- Behavior: Nodding, direct eye contact, and leaning in to the other people
- Behavior: Actively try to keep people settled, happy, and on task together

Observable signs of an Accommodator:

- Triangulates: approaches each person individually to get them to agree with each other
- Offers to do something no one else will do just to end the standoff
- Exhibits a strong desire for harmony in words or actions: *All for one, and one for all!*

Accommodator blind spots:

Accommodators fail to recognize that in all their efforts to create harmony on the team, they leave out a critical ingredient: themselves. Accommodators often don't contribute their own opinion. In the need for harmony, they short-circuit real team discussions. Accommodators over-manage the situation and get in the way of rich, real discussions that leverage the different opinions of the team members.

In the end, Accommodators often feel over-burdened and underappreciated in the attempts to manage conversations, volunteer for extra work, and take on the responsibility of settling conflict. While no one asks Accommodators to do these extra jobs, you feel compelled to volunteer because no one else is signing up.

Leadership takeaway:

When you lead as an Accommodator, you keep your real thoughts, feelings, and desires to yourself. This leads to disappointment because the team doesn't understand what you want. The team needs and misses out on your direction, opinions and critical feedback. Your growth and the team results will improve as you learn to speak up, directly give your real opinion, and tolerate the tension of people being upset.

Separator

Separators feel detached and disengaged during conflict. They think, "I'm sure they'll work it out at some point. In the meantime, I'll just check my e-mail."

This opt-out style focuses strongly on other parts of the business than the topic at hand. If you're a Separator, in the midst of tension, you ignore or block your own opinion (the ME) and the human dynamics in the room (the WE). Instead, you tend to focus on the business, but not the current business issue causing the conflict. You are most comfortable working, so when tension arises, you disengage. You pride yourself on having the right data and the correct answer. Often, the interpersonal dynamics seem unnecessary to you and, thus, better ignored.

As a Separator you prefer calm. If you can't get clarity on the current team problem, you'll focus on something else entirely, right in the midst of the meeting. You'll check e-mail or chat with the person next to you about something entirely different. You tend to think you're efficient or autonomous: "I'll just stay busy while they work it out."

When you do speak up as the Separator, you are often detached, rational, and calm. You prefer to focus on the data or bring up a completely different topic than the conflict on the table. Underlying your behavior is a desire to distance yourself from the chaos and messiness of the human dynamics. The Separator finds the inner workings of a problem to be safer ground than the inner workings of people. You appear indifferent, detached, or even dismissive.

Separator key attributes:

- Need: Clarity and calm
- Focus: On a different business problem
- Point of view: Don't reveal your opinion, and aren't curious about others' opinions
- Verbal: Rational, calm, and detached when speaking, or completely silent
- Behavior: Disengage to focus on something different

Observable signs of a Separator:

- Goes quiet in meetings
- Talks to someone about something else entirely
- Disengages and checks e-mail when disagreements arise
- Focuses on other projects unrelated to the meeting

Separator blind spots:

Separators are typically unaware how their behavior impacts the group. They essentially abandon the team, letting *them* work it out without engaging. They don't realize that developing clarity depends on their contribution even amidst human chaos.

Leadership takeaway:

As you lead and opt out as a Separator, you often focus on doing your own thing and miss the insights and input from team discussions. In your preference for calm and clarity, you tend to lead a team as a group of subject matter experts rather than driving the team to work collectively. Your growth, and the team results, will improve as you notice your tendency to work alone versus engaging in team meetings and driving collective goals.

GOOD INTENTIONS, POOR EFFECTIVENESS

The three opt-out styles are simply habits. When you feel tension in the middle of a meeting, it's easy to believe that the problem is *out there,* and that the triggers are external. But, it is your own internal discomfort and sense of being out of control that causes the greatest discomfort. These three opt-out styles are natural, ingrained responses to that discomfort— and they are typically remnants of coping methods learned growing up. The behaviors are usually automatic, unconscious, and repetitive. You may have a go-to opt-out choice, but you may dabble in all of them, depending on the circumstances.

Your intentions are pure. You want to do what is best for yourself, the team, and the project by opting out. Each opt-out style has an element of good intention:

- Being efficient, getting to the right answer quickly, and implementation
- Keeping people happy, smoothing relationships, and creating team harmony
- Staying clear, level headed, and focused on the work

Behind each of these intentions is the desire to maintain or reestablish control. The problem is, control doesn't lead to creativity; chaos does, which we know in business is counter-cultural. None of these intentions is likely to build a strong, resilient, innovative team. These opt-out styles fail to leverage the diversity of the team members by defusing the tension and ambiguity needed to create innovative solutions. These styles undermine team success. The question we pose to you is: How do you opt-out of conflict? To find out how you tend to opt out, take our online assessment at <u>www.Thriveinc.com/beautyofconflict/bonus</u>.

WHAT'S YOUR STYLE

3 Styles That Undermine Team Success

Superstar

Values: **Action and Results**
Point of View: **My Way**

Accommodator

Values: **Harmony and Relationships**
Point of View: **Your Way**

Separator

Values: **Clarity and Calm**
Point of View: **Other Way**

Don't worry, everyone opts out of conflict at times. The key is to recognize this is what you are doing and make a different choice. Here are three critical elements to support the team in using the energy of conflict:

1. Recognize your own opt-out style tendency
2. Realize opting out does not help the team get to innovative results
3. Make the shift to embrace conflict

Based on your favorite opt-out style, here are things you can say to make that shift and own what you're doing:

Superstar: "I think I have a great solution, but maybe I'm driving too fast. Let me slow down and check in with you folks."

Accommodator: "I'm uncomfortable in conflict, so I just try to fix it. Truth is, I have a different idea all together, and frankly, I didn't even bring it up because you guys keep arguing."

Separator: "I realize I'm checking out, and if I were to chime in, I'd suggest the quieter folks speak up. I'm tired of the same people making the same points."

Opting out is human. You will continue to opt out. The key is to recognize when you are optimizing your own comfort over the success of the team. That awareness allows you to make a different choice.

Once you can spot your own opt-out style, you will notice other people's as well. For a leader, this is powerful because you can keep your eye on the prize—collective results versus individual comfort. When you as a leader opt in, you will dramatically impact your team's success.

Let's explore how some leaders have dramatically increased their team's success through opting in.

CHAPTER 5
Why an Entrepreneurial Company Almost Failed

Remerge Energy was a small but fast-growing and innovative alternative energy company that had the attention of the Obama administration. The CEO, Adam, called us, his voice edged with tension. He explained that the company was four weeks into the second quarter and had already spent half of the government's Green Energy Award, which they'd been granted the previous year. At the current rate, Remerge Energy would face serious financial issues if they couldn't secure a new client or sharply reduce operational costs.

Adam clearly held his six-person leadership team in high regard. He had been appointed CEO a year earlier, after the company was awarded their first major government funding. There are three other key players in this story: Nathan, the head of research and development, was the founder and brains behind the company's prototype technology. Britney, the newest team member and head of sales and marketing, had been brought in by Adam to drive Remerge Energy's sales growth. Tom, head of operations, came aboard shortly after Nathan started the company.

Adam had tried his best to get his entire team to work well together, but his method of leadership wasn't creating the teamwork or business results he hoped for. He needed the team to be aligned.

In our initial conversation with Adam, it was obvious he had great strategic focus. He was the voice to the angel funding investors, who remained committed in spite of less-than-stellar sales reports. But Adam's focus on funding and long-term strategy left him little time to play arbitrator between Britney, the marketing maven, and Nathan, the technical genius. That job was left to Tom, who had great relational skills, but was clearly out of his league in dealing with the horsepower of Britney and the brains of Nathan, his mentor. During that first call with Adam, we agreed to work with the leadership team.

We typically start our team engagements with a leadership team event called an off-site, which is a usually a two-day retreat, and then move to one-on-one coaching with the leader and individuals. We facilitate quarterly off-sites thereafter. The teams who do this make big leaps forward and advance their momentum through the follow-up work. Beautiful big-sky Montana was the locale for this off-site. It was mid spring and we were at a lodge on the lake.

More preliminary conversations with Adam gave us insight about the root cause of the breakdown. We were curious how things would play out at the initial off-site, and we were especially interested to see the potential style differences on the team and how well the team members understood their roles.

THE INITIAL OFF-SITE

Adam opened the off-site by explaining the importance of this gathering. The focus, he said, was to uncover why they were so far off the financial plan. Moving forward, he wanted the team to figure out how to both increase funding and win sales.

Rather than wait for the agenda item, Tom, head of operations, spoke. "When we got the funding, we started down this road of scaling up from the prototype to the new larger site system because Britney has been focused on large customers. Plus, we have been implementing new design features to improve the system. Operations has been struggling to keep up, and I know our overtime costs have been higher. I am sure we are running over the original budget. However, I am trying to keep a balance to ensure we are ready for both the new site and Nathan's new design features. Both are exciting opportunities for us." Tom was always positive and determined to make everyone happy.

Britney chimed in, "Adam, I realize I am also over budget. I hired marketing and sales consultants to pull together a top-notch portfolio so that we could impress larger clients and land our second site implementation. I need to ensure we'll be on track to get more clients and funding this year."

Nathan, who was typing on his laptop, shook his head and mumbled.

CrisMarie spoke up, "Nathan we didn't hear you, and we'd like to. First though, we agreed no laptops in the meeting. Are you willing to close it and tell us what you said?"

We think it is crucial that people give full focus in the meeting, especially given the logistics of assembling the team for two days. And we prefer to hear the under-the-breath comments rather than let people stay silent. At least we knew Nathan was not completely disengaged. He was listening, even if he wasn't all in at that point.

Nathan sighed, slowly closed his computer, gave CrisMarie a look, and then shifted his glare to Britney. "What I said was, 'Of course she needed outside consultants.'"

Britney spoke up with more energy this time, looking at Nathan. "Listen, I needed a team that could pull together an accurate picture of the success and highlight the potential of the prototype for a variety of potential customers. When I asked you, you handed me a manual that only a physicist would understand. I can't use that to sell to clients. Plus, you're keeping operations so busy implementing all your new features that they were unavailable. I had to do it myself, so I brought in resources!" She sat back, arms folded.

Tom was clearly uncomfortable. He leaned forward, wanting to step in and defend both positions. "Look, I think we can agree that any new client is going to love all the new features. And Britney, I also understand translating Nathan's ideas is not easy and that I haven't been helping."

Adam sighed, "Look you guys, I am out on the road trying to keep our investors happy. I need more from each of you. Britney, these outside resources are expensive, and Tom, I wonder why you aren't able to provide some of the resources Britney needs."

Britney sat up straighter. "Look, Adam, every time we had our one-on-ones, you made it clear that you wanted sales and it was my job to create them. I talked to you about the importance of pulling together a successful portfolio, and you gave me the go-ahead. So I gathered the resources that were available and got it done."

Adam looked confused and turned toward Nathan. "I'm surprised you didn't provide more inside help for the sales portfolio."

Tom interjected, "I think Nathan's focus has been on the new designs, and it was probably my job to work more closely with Britney."

Nathan pulled out his phone apparently scrolling through his email, "Don't blame yourself, Tom," he replied. "The reason I didn't help is because Britney's plan is ridiculous. She completely focused on the wrong target market!"

Clearly, we were right in the middle of an oh, sh*t! moment that had been brewing for months. People were resorting to their preferred opt-out styles.

When an oh, sh*t! moment surfaces, it is easy to focus on the money or whatever the business issue is. But frankly, that is rarely the *root* of the problem; it's almost always a symptom. Going right to the business issue may lead to some resolution, but it won't likely be the most creative, innovative or sustainable solution. Other issues are bound to arise if the underlying dynamic is not resolved.

SHIFTING GEARS

Since the issue was on the table, we asked that the team pivot and focus on the healthy side of the business before trying to resolve the specific business issue. We assured the team that our intention was aligned with Adam's, and we would address the business issue by lunchtime. We also requested that all electronic devices be turned off during the team meeting.

Both Britney and Nathan pushed back—especially Nathan on the electronics. Adam spoke up, his voice firm. "This is critical for our business," he said. "It's important that we all fully participate so we stop arguing and start finding solutions." Everyone was on board.

We presented our *Path to Collective Creativity* team model, which maps out how teams create oh, sh*t! moments, the ways people inadvertently undermine team success with their favorite opt-out style, and the three keys to opt in and engage collective team brilliance. To find out how you tend to opt out, take our online assessment at www.Thriveinc.com/beautyofconflict/bonus.

Adam spoke up seconds after we covered the opt-out styles. "Look, I will start out by saying I think I may have been too engaged with investors and needed to get more involved in listening and working onsite with you guys. I'm guessing it's my Superstar style and possibly some Separator."

We let Adam know right then and there that he was doing a great job modeling real-time vulnerability, opening the door for others to do the same.

Tom spoke up next. "Look, I feel torn between you guys. I want to do what's best for the company, but I think I am too busy making you both happy. Britney, I do worry that you don't have the same underlying values and vision as Nathan, yet frankly, without you, all of Nathan's grand ideas aren't going anywhere. Nathan, you are brilliant, but I really need you to stop tweaking the system."

Tom, as the Accommodator, had taken on the role of keeping both Nathan and Britney happy at the cost of himself. He had been managing the tension between Nathan and Britney through one-off meetings and assigning his team to do tasks for both as best they could.

Tom knew that Adam wanted Nathan and Britney to work together and for each to weigh in on plans for the new client direction. He was at the end of his ability to navigate their different styles and strategies. In addition, he was not letting either know what he needed—he omitted the ME.

Britney, as the Superstar, was doing what she was asked to do. She had strong ideas, so when Nathan was too busy and didn't have resources to offer, she got the job done using her own resources. Though she did approach Nathan, he was distant, and she assumed she had to do it herself. Britney was confident in the ME and thought she had the *right* strategy to solve the problem. However, she omitted the WE and did not check out what was going on with Nathan. She didn't ask the reason for his lack of cooperation, nor did she tell Adam how she was solving the problem.

Nathan's Separator opt-out style came into play as he avoided the conflict with Britney's desire to get new, broader-range clients. As the Separator, he focused on his own area, research and development. He was uncomfortable with many of Britney's ideas and client choices and, therefore, ignored her request for help. Meanwhile, Nathan assumed Adam would get Britney aligned; Nathan would just wait until she was up to speed, then he would reengage. The problem was his team member also needed some of his resources to move forward.

Nathan left out both the ME (by not speaking up about his concerns with Britney's approach) and the WE (by not exploring what Britney was up to with her plans). Instead, he put his head down and focused on the business, but only in his specific area. As a result, he justified his position that Britney was a bad hire.

All these choices to opt out happened repeatedly over the course of a few months. Any one of these efforts has merits, such as making sure work gets done, albeit in silos, or keeping harmony on the team. But by not directly dealing with the real conflict between team members, these opt-out styles actually undermined collective effort and, more importantly, the overall business results! This stalled the forward movement of the organization and created a drain on finances. The right conversations did not happen because people avoided conflict instead of putting it to use.

Fortunately for the team, at the end of the morning of day one, they were engaged in our *Path to Collective Creativity Team* model. With Adam's willingness to open with vulnerability, and Tom's stepping up to acknowledge the impact Britney and Nathan had on him, the groundwork was in place for Nathan and Britney to engage fully with each other. Once they identified their own opt-out styles, it was easy to create a space for more dialogue and check out some of the assumptions.

Nathan let Britney know his deeper concerns that her choice to go after big oil companies felt like a misalignment in values. Britney was surprised and shared that she wasn't going after big oil because she was aligned with them. She actually thought Nathan's approach and efforts could have a significant impact and influence the oil companies to reconsider environmentally friendly alternatives as a part of their portfolio. Getting that misunderstanding cleared up was monumental.

By the end of the off-site, the team made significant shifts in how they did business. Nathan agreed to work with Britney by going to the next potential client site. The two laid out a plan with Tom to use internal resources to create the input and map for future client engagement.

Once the leadership team was aligned, specifically Tom, Britney, and Nathan, we suggested the team communicate their clarity to the rest of the 80-person organization at an all-hands meeting, which we would facilitate. The day began with team- and trust-building activities, both within the individual teams and cross-functionally. Then the entire leadership team stood to communicate their vision to the rest of the organization.

Adam spoke first. He acknowledged the team's previous lack of alignment, the impact to the organization, and the need to make it different. Nathan and Britney then openly addressed their differences and how they had come from very different directions without appreciation for the impact that might have on Tom and operations overall. In the room packed with people, you could hear a pin drop. Everyone had already been aware of this. When the two leaders acknowledged what was real, they built strong credibility.

The leadership team then talked about the new direction. Britney and Nathan presented a combined portfolio of their ideas, which reflected their collective brilliance. The room was electric with the new possibilities. We went on to facilitate some round table discussions about the key objection areas and implementation plans. The employees provided great insights and feedback to improve the plan going forward.

Nathan, Britney, and Tom communicated their vision, aligned and re-inspired. Now the company's focus was new sales and securing funding, and the employees rallied around it. Since the company was aligned from the top down, they no longer needed to spend money on operations overtime or outside sales and marketing firms. Adam could focus on securing funding and also stay more connected to what was happening back at the offices through weekly tactical and monthly strategic meetings. Over the next nine months, the company successfully secured funding, won several new clients, and increased the ROI and success of Remerge.

Do you now have a sense of the impact opting out has on the team and the business? When opt-out behaviors go unaddressed, especially on a leadership team, it can undermine an entire company. When this happens and companies fail, the newspaper headlines shout bad business strategy and poor timing—and that's accurate. However, if you examine what happened inside those board rooms, nine out of ten times the mistakes were a result of team members' opting out of the right conversations. Avoiding addressing the underlying team dysfunction wreaks havoc for the business.

It doesn't have to be this way. You, your team, and your business can increase your bottom line and your sense of satisfaction by working together.

Read on to learn how to opt-in, create more success, and increase the bottom line.

SECTION THREE
Opt In

SECTION THREE
OVERVIEW

Your team is in the midst of conflict. You've bumped into an oh, sh*t! moment. At this point, most people go on automatic pilot, choosing safe, habitual responses. We encourage you to wake up and notice this moment, because it's a crucial choice point for you and your team.

Do you opt in, or do you opt out?

Opting in creates a container in which differences can be used not as points of contention, but as invitations to more creative solutions. Opting in means stepping into the conflict, rather than avoiding it. Choosing to engage with conflict is counterintuitive and demands a tremendous amount of courage, backbone, and heart on the part of everyone involved.

So why do it? Because you and your team will reap amazingly creative, innovate, and profitable collective results!

COLLECTIVE CREATIVITY PATH

To opt in, you must be willing to show up with *vulnerability,* let down your guard, and relinquish the control that makes you feel safe. You must also choose *curiosity* and be willing to share your opinion and express genuine interest in different perspectives. While these two ingredients aren't natural in business, especially for leaders, they are learnable skills. Consistent application of vulnerability and curiosity creates a container for innovation and creativity.

When you and your team opt in and use the natural energy of conflict, you each become healthier, more engaged, and significantly more creative. Individuals start to speak up, share different points of view, express disagreement with one another—even with you, the leader—and think more creatively. Trust, connection, and curiosity grow; and everyone becomes more resilient. The team's willingness, ability, and capacity to deal with differences improve. As a result, the team finds clarity in the problem and expands the playing field of possibilities.

Rather than deferring to the leader's or loudest member's opinion, team members come up with creative solutions together. They arrive at ideas none of them considered before walking into the room. Momentum increases because people are inspired and engaged. No longer does one person have to pull the team along; they're pushing ahead together.

In this section, we provide the concepts, tools, and tips to support your choice to opt in to conflict in order to encourage clarity and collective creativity on your team. We will set the context for the following three sections: the ME, the WE, and the BUSINESS.

Read on to find out what learning to ski has to do with opting in.

CHAPTER 6
If You Can Learn to Ski, You Can Learn to Use Conflict

Come opening day of ski season on Whitefish Mountain Resort, I (Susan) plan to be skiing. Before I turned fifty, I could count on one hand the number of times I'd been to the ski hill. For years, I'd *talked* about learning to ski but had always found reasons to let my athletic successes remain in my past rather than risk something new. That is, until CrisMarie gave me ski lessons for Christmas.

There I was, the day after Christmas, in a beginner's ski class with munchkins who were half my size. These little guys were way more daring and graceful than I, and they had only half the distance to fall. Clearly, I wasn't skiing because I was a natural. No, I wanted to learn, stretch myself, and discover a new way to connect with my body, my mind, and nature. In two years, I've become better, although I'm still humbled when I venture beyond the bunny slopes.

Facing a new challenge is hard. That's why leaders often elect to stay in their comfort zones and have their teams stay right there with them. The fear of mastering something new prevents reaching for and getting to an individual's and team's best next work.

How does this happen? Leaders, and teams as a result, get caught between *defending* and *growing*—opting out or opting in. Often, they don't even notice what's happening. This presents both a human paradox and a choice point: should you defend the status quo (opt out) or grow (opt in)? For me, that meant: do I stay comfortable in my past successes (stay off the slopes), or grow by trying something new (learn to ski)? I'm glad I chose to opt in.

WELCOME FEAR

The first step to opting in is to understand that you *have* a choice. The next step is to develop the capacity to tolerate the tension and ambiguity (in other words, conflict), both within yourself and between yourself and others.

One of the greatest barriers to this is fear. Most of us fear conflict. Yes, even the toughest of us. As a result, we avoid it. We discussed avoidance tactics in depth in the previous section. In this chapter, we'll explore some ways people welcome those fears and engage with conflict.

A necessary stage of risk taking is saying and doing things that may disrupt the good vibes. Speaking up, whether through words or actions, can create distance and awkwardness. Some risky examples include:

- Saying no.
- Giving a teammate feedback on an unproductive behavior.
- Being vulnerable: "I don't know how to do that," "I made a mistake," or "I'm envious of your new role."
- Interrupting a rambling answer.
- Not participating in gossip between team members.

Moments of discomfort naturally arise when people work together. Most of us avoid confronting and addressing them because we're afraid of the consequences. We say things like:

> "I don't want to create a problem."

"I don't want to look weak."

"If I bring this up, it will derail our forward progress."

"I'll be rude."

"I don't want to rock the boat."

This fear and avoidance of conflict is the *human* reason why leaders and their teams settle for less than their best and most creative collective work. There is also a *business* reason.

When something is good, or good enough, it's human nature to stop taking new risks for fear of putting a damper on productivity. As people try new things, stretch, and make the mistakes that are inherent to reaching the next stage of development, efficiency typically decreases. Stalled productivity is a natural stage of learning, but one that leaders frequently downplay or find surprising.

Imagine you're leading a project team or business unit that has done great work. You know you have a solid, reliable reputation in your field. You're enjoying great benefits because of it. Why take a chance of disruption to seek something new?

Business as usual is highly seductive, particularly if that business has solid success. But people doing the same work over and over, even if it's great work, will get bored. Motivation will suffer. Great leaders know this is the time to take action. But it's not always easy to step out of your comfort zone to make the necessary changes.

There's that paradox again! Should you defend the status quo (opt out), or grow (opt in)? Should you continue doing what you've always done (opt out), or welcome your fears (opt in)?

The creative process demands risks and mistakes. It flows, and it stalls. Handling the flow and stalls requires a tolerance for tension and ambiguity as well as the strength to welcome fear. A creative leader achieves this by trusting that a pause or dip in productivity will end, and something new will emerge.

Tolerating the ups and downs of the creative process is hard enough solo, but even harder on a team. When a team navigates a learning curve, members experience more conflict. They doubt and second-guess themselves and one another. When they keep those doubts and fears underground and unacknowledged, the team members reflect the very fears they want to avoid.

Remember the two magic qualities? To reach creative potential, a team must be *vulnerable*, which means failing and recovering. The team must be *curious* about everything that comes to the table. From that, a team's collective wisdom emerges!

I could have said a polite 'thanks' to CrisMarie for the ski lessons and then never ventured to the mountain. When I saw the pint-size skiers in my class, I could have given up then and there. But I didn't. I faced my fears and pushed myself to do something different. I got a little banged up along the way, but I pushed past it to discover something I now truly love.

Opt in to your fears! Don't be afraid to fail. Learn how to get back up and go again.

Let's see exactly how vulnerability and curiosity can help you make the choice to opt in and grow.

CHAPTER 7
Two Magic Ingredients That Drive Team Creativity

A few years back, we worked with an information technology company that had seen steady success and had acquired a smaller company. As a result of the acquisition, the president of the small company, Jane, joined the executive team.

Frank, the CEO, requested our help with onboarding Jane. When he said more than once that Jane's style wasn't working on the team, and "she needs to learn how we work around here," we got the impression that rather than onboarding Jane, Frank wanted to mute her or change her. We agreed to begin by working with the team for two days.

On the first afternoon, we discussed the company's new product strategy. Jane vehemently disagreed with the rest of the team. Suddenly, three team members were on their feet, yelling and pointing at her. We were shocked by their immediate response, and we quickly called a time-out. We encouraged them to remember the two magic ingredients we'd introduced earlier in the day, vulnerability and curiosity.

One teammate, Joe, shifted his perspective and became vulnerable.

"Listen," he said to Jane. "I'm frustrated with you because it seems like you always disagree with us. I don't even listen to you anymore because I'm pissed." He paused, a bit taken aback by his own outspokenness.

Susan nodded at him in encouragement and said, "Keep going, Joe."

Joe waited a beat, then continued. "Okay, I want to try to be curious," he said, then got up, slowly walked to Jane, and sat next to her. "I have no clue why you're so passionate. I don't know what you're thinking. Help me understand."

Jane became equally vulnerable. "This has been hard for me," she said. "You folks don't see the world like I do."

Jane explained her point of view, and the energy in the room completely shifted. We could see the lights come on as Joe finally understood Jane. The discussion continued, and the team designed a completely new product strategy, incorporating both Jane's perspective and what they wanted. This session was a catalyst for growth, and along with hard work, they catapulted into the top-three slot in their industry.

As Joe and Jane learned, the task of working as a team requires holding the tension of belief in your opinion while being equally interested in the opinions of your team members. Great teamwork involves a willingness to have ideas challenged, knocked down, and possibly tossed out. The choice to opt in to this wrestling process allows new ideas to emerge and creativity to flourish.

Through our work with partnerships, teams, and businesses, we've found that vulnerability and curiosity, when practiced and applied by even just one person, have the potential to transform a team in an instant. These two qualities help people work with and use the tension that surfaces in challenging situations.

LET'S GET VULNERABLE

Not too many people like the concept of vulnerability. Plus, in business? You've got to be kidding! Business is the realm of invincibility, right?

Not when you're working on a team. If you want results, the strength of your relationship with your team matters, and vulnerability is key to growing those relationships. Being vulnerable doesn't mean being weak. Instead, it's the willingness to expose yourself to danger. Not for the faint of heart, eh?

Vulnerability is taking the risk to be real and honest about what's happening for you inside; to reveal what you really think, feel, and want in the moment. To be vulnerable:

Reveal what isn't being said. This sounds deceptively simple, but it can be hard to do. Share a different opinion—dare to reveal that the emperor wears no clothes.

Speak up about what's happening inside of you. Tell others if you're uncomfortable, angry, worried, or don't know the answer.

Drop the effort to look good, smart, or in charge. Instead, let your teammates see that you're human. Own that you don't understand, are sorry, or made a mistake.

Acknowledge that there isn't a *right* answer, or that you don't know what the answer is. It's natural to want to know exactly what to do or say, because having the answer makes people feel safe and secure. While leaders want to be the ones to provide answers, vulnerability requires them to admit when they don't know.

Vulnerability can be messy. Yet we've experienced time and time again that when one person has the courage to be vulnerable, to share what no one else has the courage to say, the energy of the room shifts immediately. The conversation gets real. People stop trying to *manage* the situation, simply hoping they can escape and start generating real, creative solutions.

Vulnerability has other benefits, too. When you are vulnerable, you:

Shift from managing the world around you to landing squarely in your own shoes, which has tremendous power.

Gain the ability and courage to move forward proactively, because you're no longer holding anything back.

Have more access to your creativity, because you're not wasting energy covering up what is truly happening inside of you—your thoughts, feelings, and wants.

Vulnerability also has advantages for the team as a whole. The team:

Builds trust, because people trust others who say what they really think, feel, and want.

Gets to the right results, because more of the story is out on the table.

Arrives at collective creativity, enabling forward progress.

What is the business reason to be real and vulnerable? Vulnerability is a magic ingredient to cut through the niceties and get to the real conversation. When you as a leader are willing to be vulnerable, you build trust and loyalty. Your conversations save time and drive innovative business solutions that increase your profitability. It's a small price to pay!

BE JUDGMENTAL - REALLY!

Despite the benefits of vulnerability, people avoid it. This is partially because they don't want to come across as judgmental. Saying what's real often means directly sharing judgments about people and their work.

But here's the reality: You are judgmental. We all are. Being judgmental serves us; it's how we make meaning of our world. In fact, your judgment is one of your greatest gifts, and it's likely why you got hired.

Your judgment or opinion is a combination of your abilities in imagination, creativity, and discernment. Judgments are reflective of how you put your world together. It's what makes you unique, valuable, and a smart addition to a team. Being honest with yourself and others about your judgments is part of being vulnerable.

The problem isn't judgments; the problem lies in *righteous attachment*. Righteous attachment to judgment kills creativity and innovation on teams. We call this the right-wrong trap. When you're righteously attached to your judgments, you're fixed in your own position. You're thinking in black and white terms, stuck in your perspective. You won't see another way.

Conversely, healthy teams welcome and value differing judgments and opinions. In a trusting environment, teammates speak up when they think others are being ineffective, making a mistake, or sharing an idea that, well, sucks.

Yes, revealing and hearing judgment creates conflict. It's uncomfortable, painful, and awkward. But holding back your judgment and opinion not only dampens your team's creativity, it also diminishes its effectiveness. Even if you don't speak up, the judgment and conflict is still there; it's just underground and unused.

When you share your judgment directly as just what it is—only your judgment, not reality—you and your team gain the chance to use the energy of conflict. By sharing your outlook, someone else can provide you with a different perspective, new information, or the backstory for his or her motivation for a differing judgment.

When speaking your judgments, use 'I' statements. Own it as *your* view of the world, not *the* view of the world, and ask for the other person's take. Imagine sharing your judgments like this:

"I don't think your approach is sound, so help me understand how you got there."

"Based on the data I've seen, my story is that your approach won't work. Can you help me understand where I'm wrong?"

"I don't have confidence that your approach will work. I've been hesitant to tell you, but I want to know what you think."

The second halves of these sentences are key, as they reveal curiosity. And that's the second magic ingredient.

BE CURIOUS

Where there's conflict, there's always a choice point for those involved: do you defend, or do you get curious?

What do we mean by *get curious*? We mean pause, consider, and honestly reflect on what is being presented other than your viewpoint. Even if someone else's idea seems insane to you, they likely came to it with good reason. The challenge is to pause and try to understand—not necessarily agree on—how the other person came to that *crazy* position.

It's not easy. When you're passionate about something and have a strong opinion, it's difficult to pause and listen, much less reflect and consider. Still, whenever we do this or witness our clients' curiosity, it's powerful. The energy in the room shifts. We've seen it happen over and over again.

The key is to become curious about the other person's point of view after you own up to yours. Curiosity opens the space to develop something new, and unlocks the door to use judgment and conflict for creativity and innovation.

You don't have to let go of your judgments or opinions. Curiosity means having your judgments *and* being open and interested in a different perspective. Being curious means:

- Considering that there may be more than one right way, reality, or answer.
- Stopping the fight for your *right* way and being open to the ideas of others.
- Taking an interest in how the other person came to his or her conclusion.
- Listening with the willingness to be influenced.

Some phrases that help demonstrate curiosity and elicit another's response are:

"Help me understand how you got there."
"Why is this so important to you?"
"What is driving your strong conviction?"
"Can you help me understand where I'm wrong?"
"Wow! That is very different from my view. How'd you get there?"

The benefits of being curious include:

- Getting outside of your own story, which opens a greater pool of information to generate creative ideas;
- Strengthening the team's learning and growth;
- Making the other person feel heard and considered;
- Shifting the energy from defense to cooperation, opening the door to new, creative possibilities;
- Transitioning the focus of the team from power struggles to idea expansion.

A leader's job isn't to have the right answer, but to create the space for the project, team, or organization to move forward. When even one person listens to and reflects on the opposing opinion of a peer with genuine curiosity, the change in the room is palpable. That combination of vision, opinion, and passion, when combined with curiosity, leads the entire team to new possibilities. That's the role of a healthy dose of curiosity.

VULNERABILITY + CURIOSITY = CREATIVITY

When teams are vulnerable and curious, they use the natural energy of conflict to recognize that it isn't my way or your way, but a whole new way. New ideas emerge. Instead of a fight, there is magic.

It starts with people opting in, becoming vulnerable, and revealing what they really think, feel, and want. This allows for a free flow of opinions (judgments) combined with curiosity (not righteousness or defensiveness). The result? A team that uses the energy of conflict to become smarter and highly innovative.

Teams that master the use of vulnerability and curiosity produce creative and innovative solutions not just once, but repeatedly. They bounce back from setbacks and failure. People feel engaged and fulfilled, and they have more fun. It's probably no surprise that vulnerability and curiosity work wonders in personal relationships too.

Either of these qualities can instantly transform a team in conflict. Put them together and the team makes a quantum leap forward. It only takes one individual. Are you willing to be that person?

If you want to learn more about the combination of vulnerability and curiosity and the power it creates on teams, check out our TEDx Talk *Conflict: Use It, Don't Defuse It!* on YouTube or at www.Thriveinc.com/beautyofconflict.

Read on to see what horses can teach you about conflict.

CHAPTER 8
What Horses Taught Me about Conflict

Because we urge you to *use* conflict, you may think we're fight fans. We're not! There is a clear distinction between fighting and using conflict. In fact, they're at different ends of the same continuum.

Let's back up and discuss fighting, and even flight-ing, and the opt-out styles.

You may remember that the superstar opt-out style includes behavior that could be interpreted as fighting. Superstars think their opinion is right, they want to move the meeting along, and they are dismissive of other peoples' reservations. Separators, on the other hand, demonstrate behavior that could be interpreted as flight. They disengage in the topic, walk out of the room, and don't participate in team activities. Accommodators have a different flavor of flight behavior. They omit their own opinion, they ask questions, and they short-circuit the disagreement by changing the topic.

All of these opt-out styles are on one end of the continuum. Opting in with conflict is on the other.

FIGHTING AND FLIGHT-ING VERSUS USING CONFLICT

FIGHT — USE

Fighting/Flight-ing ⟵————⟶ **Using Conflict**

Fighting and flight-ing are one-dimensional. Use of conflict is multidimensional and creates the space for both the leader and team to show up fully.

Susan coaches star performers in an organization who get results, and who run over others in the process. When she works with these clients, they initially say, "I don't know what the problem is. I'm doing my job and getting the results." Their point is valid. Organizations tend to reward star players for strong business results and either overlook or hope the associated aggressive behaviors will eventually shift.

The Superstar leaders she coaches have strong opinions and believe they are right. Day-to-day they tell people what to do; they focus on getting things done. If someone doesn't perform, they go around them. If that person is a direct report, these leaders are quick to fire them, more so than are other styles of leader. This aggressive tendency isn't all bad. It drives action. But left unchecked it undermines the leader, the team, and the organization overall. Action for action's sake is not always, or even usually, the best strategy. Without slowing down to consider the input of those around them, this leader can accomplish a lot, but undermine the business overall because he gets results in a silo. He misses how his action impacts others. This leader thwarts the development of the collective team intelligence.

To shift from fight behaviors to using conflict, this leader needs to be aware of the impact his behavior has on others. It is good to start with people the leader respects, because they are more likely to listen and recognize that they may not be right. This helps the leader develop the muscle of curiosity.

CrisMarie often works with leaders who were previously high performers, but now, for some reason, struggle. It could be that their confidence has waned, they are not being assertive, or they hold on to poor performers too long. These leaders are generally well liked by their direct reports and are themselves very hard working. However, their own performance slips because they don't stand up for their own point of view, they say yes to requests for work, they take on too much, and they keep giving their direct reports another chance.

This type of leader has more of a flight style, and when issues arise, she resorts to asking questions or minimizing tension through avoidance, using diplomacy, or being nice and polite. Again, these skills are useful in relationship building, but by themselves, they do not create success in the workplace. This leader is not serving herself, the team, or the organization.

To shift from flight behaviors to using conflict, this leader needs to develop the ability and courage to speak up with her own honest, frank opinion, and engage in dialogue, tolerating others being upset. Yes, this will be challenging and uncomfortable at first. However, when she can stand forth and voice her opinion, she regains confidence. Then she is more effective at giving feedback to poor performers, and if the behavior doesn't improve, she will make the call to finally let a poor performer go.

At team meetings, the combination of the fight and flight behaviors is unproductive. Even though some team members speak up, it's often by interrupting or talking over other people, with little pause or reflection of anyone else's input. Those who choose flight are either silent or simply managing the tension by smoothing over the disagreements. When we work with teams like this, the person who has fight behaviors tells us, "Oh, we have great conflict and debate in our meetings!" We don't hear anything from people with flight behaviors until we take a break. Then they tell us privately, "Our meetings have terrible conflict. No one listens to each other."

These teams show evidence of conflict, but they are not using that energy for collective brilliance. Instead, the loudest idea wins, and it's a one-dimensional solution. It is important to note here that a fight behavior is just another coping style for dealing with the building tension and ambiguity in the room. It does not indicate the ability to leverage differences to develop a greater team intelligence. You may be surprised to learn that fighting is still a conflict-avoidance strategy.

The team dysfunction is not due only to the fight behaviors. People with both fight and flight behaviors are equally responsible for the dysfunctional dynamic. It is the leader's job to shift the dynamic to help the team engage and use conflict for collective results.

Let's reiterate; even *we* don't love conflict. What we *do* love is the perfect storm that occurs when vision, opinion, and passion come together. Handled correctly, that combination is fertile ground for creativity, innovation, and aha moments. The key? You guessed it: opting in to the pressure of conflict and allowing the tension to build. Let us use horses to demonstrate.

HORSES AND EMOTIONAL INTELLIGENCE

Susan is a certified Equus Coach, expert at using horses for leadership development. She also uses horses with entire teams and continues to be awed at the impact on individuals and groups when working with a horse.

On a physical level, horses are gorgeous, powerful, and neurologically quite sensitive. On a spiritual level, well, there's a reason these animals appear in so many mythological stories and are considered symbols of mystery and majesty. But what really surprises us, and why Susan uses them in working with people, is their keen sense of emotional intelligence. This makes them excellent mentors for reading and working with conflict.

Horses are prey animals. They never look for a fight. Instead, they constantly scan and read their environment for signs of danger. They have a sophisticated zone of awareness, meaning they notice the instant someone comes into the pasture. They read that person behaviorally, energetically, and emotionally from a significant distance and make instantaneous decisions to move, flee, or be on alert.

As that person moves in closer, she enters the horse's zone of pressure. The horse goes on high alert. You would think the horse, as a prey animal, would run away. However, under pressure, a horse will lean in.

This instinct comes from years of *survival of the fittest.* The equine species learned that when under attack, or when a predator gets its jaws into the horse's underbelly, if the horse runs, it will tear their skin and expose their intestines.[2] The horse will likely die. The horse leans in to prevent the predator from ripping its skin. For horses, opting in is lifesaving.

For years, we've encouraged leaders and teams to do the same—stop fighting and start using conflict. We have been met with skepticism because people typically believe that to survive conflict requires pushing away the attacker. No way do they want to lean into that enemy!

However, as we've discussed throughout this section, we've found over and over again that when you are curious about what the other person has to say, rather than pulling away, everything shifts. It's no longer your idea versus their idea. A whole new set of ideas, solutions, and possibilities emerges.

Of course, people aren't horses. Humans have a natural tendency to avoid, deny, or bully through issues. But if you want to reap the benefits of conflict, you would do well to learn from these amazing animals. There are three steps to opting in to conflict, which we've drawn straight from the behavior of horses.

1. Find Your Zone of Awareness

Notice when you begin to pick up signals of the energy and behavior of people around you. Indicators that people are escalating into opting out can be nonverbal:

- They stand up to make a point
- They look elsewhere or turn their body away
- They lean back, arms crossed
- They leave the room

Or the signs can be verbal:

- They raise their voice
- They repeat a point
- They continuously interrupt
- They go silent

Practice looking for these signals early on, before the situation gets into the zone of pressure or escalation.

When a horse wants a relationship with you, he lets you know when you're not being clear or when he needs more space. He ignores ambivalent signs and signals and waits for clear ones, or he moves away if you try to come too close.

2. Don't Assume—Test and Check

When reading signs and signals from others in your zone of awareness, don't assume you know their intentions. Horses test and check. For you, explicitly testing and checking can be as simple as saying, "I notice you've repeated the same point several times. I'm wondering if you're uncomfortable or don't think I'm listening to you."

3. Under Pressure, Opt In

A horse under pressure literally leans in, putting its weight against another animal's body. It doesn't flee or fight; it surrenders. Surrender is helpful in our human interactions, too. In that zone of pressure or escalation, when the situation is most tense, what if you surrender, suspend your own agenda, get vulnerable, and be curious about the other person's point of view? We think you'll be surprised by the impact you can make doing something horses have done successfully for more than 10,000 years.[3]

Prey vs Predator

Here's the deal: unlike horses, humans aren't prey animals. Our instinctive nature allows for fight or flight: prey or predator. However, we do have the capacity to develop choice and go against our instinct, to lean in and engage our hearts and minds.

Humans in disagreement can get caught in the fight-or-flight reflex. For you as a leader, that undermines you, the team, and the bottom-line business results. In your fight-or-flight mode, you don't think clearly, don't have access to your best resources, and won't support the development of the team's collective intelligence. Learn to develop your emotional intelligence, just like a horse. Build the zone of awareness of yourself and others, be curious, and check out what is happening with others in the room.

Next up, we'll take this out of the pasture and into the office to explore the issue of getting and keeping employees engaged.

CHAPTER 9
Shift Employees from Disengagement to Active Engagement

Max was the chief information officer for a national financial company. When we first heard from him, his Gallup employee engagement scores showed two actively engaged employees to every one actively disengaged employee. Not good. A favorable score is a ratio of twelve actively engaged to one actively disengaged. Clearly, Max had a problem.

Larry, his VP of human resources, told us the story of when Max first got the news and made the decision to call us. Here's what happened:

Max was furious about the findings. "Two to one! Really? That's horrible!"

Larry, who had coordinated the survey, was responsible for giving Max honest feedback. "Look, it *is* bad, really bad. And frankly, that's the overall organization. Your executive team's results may be even worse."

Max stood up. "My team works hard. No way are they that disengaged!" He wasn't ready to entertain the possibility that the root of the problem was at the top.

Larry watched quietly.

Max paced back and forth behind his desk. "Hell, we're in the process of changing an entire technology culture at this company. I don't have time to deal with this issue right now. I'm doing my best to get employees to commit to new IT systems and let go of the legacy ones. That's really what we need to be focused on, not this people stuff!"

Larry spoke up. "Yes, you're making a big business shift, and I'm sure that's contributing to the engagement issue, but I've been talking to you about this for more than a year now." Larry paused and looked Max in the eye. "Max, there are some unspoken issues on your team. You can keep looking further down the organization, but I'm not sure the engagement problem will be solved until you deal with your own team's discontent." Larry leaned back, his body stiff, bracing for Max's reaction.

Max looked down, shaking his head. "Damn it, Larry," he said, dejected. "I hate to admit it, but you may be right."

To Max's credit, he took Larry's advice to work on his team. When we got the call from Max, he'd already primed the pump with his team to get some straight goods about the current issues. What he learned was unsettling. Three of his ten direct reports were quite clear that their issues were with Stan, Max's genius IT right-hand man.

Stan had been working for Max for fifteen years, ten of those within the current organization. Stan really was a genius, but he also had a forceful, arrogant leadership style. Still, Max couldn't believe that at this level of the organization, leadership style should be a serious problem. While he'd been working with Stan to soften his approach with the team, the truth was Max valued Stan's strong personality.

THE INTERVENTION

Our standard practice is to start with the leader or start with the team. In this case we started with the team in a two-day off-site and planned for a longer-term approach after those initial two days. Max's objectives during that first session were clear: he wanted this off-site to help his team deal more directly with Stan and other aggressive leaders, and he planned to focus his people on the company's strategic shift.

We agreed with Max that strong personality types shouldn't be a reason for breakdowns in communication, and we assured him the strategic discussion would be a major focus of the two days. We also let Max know we weren't convinced Stan was the main issue, or that his team's passive style was at fault.

Max opened the first day by making it clear he wanted everyone's input and the intention was to operate as a team. If there were issues with his leadership, he wanted that on the table.

The first day started out well—a bit too well. Some folks clearly stayed quiet as Stan dominated the discussion of strategy. It wasn't until the late afternoon that things finally heated up. We dove into some of the key issues regarding the lack of adoption of the new cloud system.

Stan jumped in. "This isn't a systems issue," he said, his tone assertive. "It's a training problem."

"Stan, I don't think so," Colin, one of the newer members of the leadership team, replied. "Your department didn't take enough time to gather the needs of a few of the business units. I think if we step back and deal with some of these smaller but unique requirements from the business units, we'll have much more buy-in across the company."

"Damn it, this isn't my team's problem!" Stan shot back. He turned saying, "Max, you know we've spent hours listening to all the requests, and frankly, most of that was a waste of time!"

"Stan, bring it down a notch," Max said. "I get that this is a difficult conversation, but we want to keep this conversation happening." He turned, saying, "Colin, look, I appreciate that people are upset with not getting everything they want, but Stan has a point. His people can't answer to everything. I'm not sure I agree with your concerns."

Colin went quiet. Silence hung in the room for several moments.

Susan interjected. "Colin, what's up? You had a point, and now you're just letting it go because Max doesn't agree?"

Colin sounded defeated. "Look, it's just not worth it."

"What's really bugging you, Colin?" she asked.

Colin paused, then steeled his resolve. "Well, here's the thing. Whenever one of us disagrees with Stan, it doesn't take long for Max to step in and agree with Stan. I don't really like that Stan gets upset, but what's even harder is that the alignment between Max and Stan is so tight that this (he made a wide circle with his hand, gesturing toward the others in the room) isn't a team. Those two are the team." He waved his hand in the direction of Max and Stan.

"Wait a minute," Max jumped in.

Susan interrupted. "Max, I'm going to stop you for a moment. This seems like a pretty honest and vulnerable statement from Colin. Are you sure you want to cut him off?"

Max stopped. There was a long pause. He finally spoke to Colin. "So, you think I always take Stan's side?"

Silence again. Everyone remained quiet, waiting for Colin's reply.

Finally, he responded, "Yes. I know Stan is great at what he does, but it'd be nice to be heard and maybe get a moment of consideration." Colin's statement was strong, but he delivered it levelly.

Max seemed to be listening, but the silence continued. Tension filled the room until Max said tersely, "I'm going to have to think on that."

Day one ended in discomfort.

THE TURNING POINT

First thing the next morning, Max stood up and addressed the team. "Look, I've been giving this a lot of thought. What you need to know is that I have a long history with Stan. I also know I like the way he thinks, and that he takes action." Stan took a breath and looked up, relieved.

"However," Max continued, "I think this is a problem. Colin, I appreciate your candor. I want you and anyone else on the team to speak up and tell me when I'm shutting down alternative ideas or teamwork because of a close working relationship with Stan. I also want to say this is not Stan's problem. I know some issues have come up for folks working with Stan, but now I'm wondering if I am the bigger issue."

Suddenly, the door was open to the tough but necessary conversation. Team members proceeded to give Max direct and challenging feedback. They agreed that a major piece of the team issue was more related to Max's alignment than Stan's aggressive style. Each person agreed to be more direct and responsible in dealing with Stan, if Max agreed to let them call him out when he so quickly aligned with Stan and stopped ongoing dialogue.

For the remainder of the off-site, the team enjoyed healthy dialogue about getting full buy-in and support for the company's cultural shift.

Toward the end of day two, the team gave Stan direct feedback whenever he would either start bullying an employee or try to recruit Max to his position. Stan seemed to take it in. We knew the team was taking a critical step forward. Members of the team thought their work was done.

But it wasn't that simple. We returned for a tune-up a month later and witnessed another critical conversation. This time, it was Max who made it clear that his first priority was the team, and he didn't think Stan had that same intention. Stan didn't take this well.

Within the next two months, Stan moved on to a new position in another large company. It wasn't easy for Max to lose Stan, but we continued to work with the team over the next year. They became fully engaged and creative in implementing the new strategy. On a coaching call Max told us, "To tell you the truth, Stan was so brilliant I had my doubts we'd be as good without him. But wow! Having an entire team operating on all cylinders has exponentially improved our performance. I never thought it was possible. I am blown away!"

A year later, with the team fully engaged and the culture shifting, the question still remained: How would this change organizational engagement levels? The annual Gallup engagement scores one year later were better: five actively engaged employees to one actively disengaged. It still wasn't up to twelve-to-one industry standards, but it was headed in the right direction.

We continued to work with the team and company for the next two years. When we last spoke, the organization's Gallup engagement scores had skyrocketed to seventeen actively engaged employees to one actively disengaged! *Using* conflict rather than *fighting* not only provided the needed energy to build a solid leadership team for the organization, but also supplied the critical shift to turn around organizational engagement.

A LEADER'S CHOICE

Max had to make some tough choices.

Team transformation comes out of fire, from the aftermath of a crisis, a blow up, or a leader who has encountered a *dark night of the soul.*

Max needed to face his own *dark night of the soul* and recognize how his relationship with Stan and his behaviors with the team limited the energy and success of the team.

He also needed to give his team permission to be messy and put the real issues on the table.

Too often a leader unwittingly defuses the tension by:

1. Determining the right answer, primarily through logic, reason, and efficiency.
2. Cutting off discussion and taking things *off-line* when people get too emotional.
3. Managing strong personalities through one-on-one conversations.
4. Listening to the loudest or the favorite voice, the one whose thoughts are usually the same as the leader's.
5. Declaring oneself as the leader and forcing a direction.

Max had spent months doing just that without realizing the impact it had on the team.

His team needed an environment in which they could all wrestle, declare, inquire, make mistakes, listen, and learn. Sometimes the team needs to safely explode so they can transform from the ashes. When a team has this contained space within which to engage, and when the explosion is invited rather than defused, an alchemical process creates innovation.

We'll dive more deeply into this as we move into the ME. But let's recap with a few key things Max did really well to shift from opting out to opting in, things you can do to be a better leader!

When team transformation is the goal, here's how a leader can opt in:

1. Be human and acknowledge conflict. You are the model. If you acknowledge when you're uncomfortable in the tension and ambiguity, others learn they're not alone.

2. Don't go for the quick fix. The drive for efficiency is born from the discomfort of not having the answer or a fear of looking bad.

3. Get out of the right-wrong trap. Yes, we all want to be right, but do you want to be right more than you want to succeed?

4. Check for conflict. If you see people disengage, check it out. Encourage people to speak up, to have different opinions, and to hang in for the long haul.

5. Listen to the naysayer with interested curiosity. Even when you think a team member is a pain in the butt, step into his shoes and see the world from his point of view. You might be surprised what you find when you get out of your own way.

What have you got to lose? Similar to Max, you might be surprised by the big leap your team makes when you take the risk, let them get messy, and use the conflict to transform.

Read on to learn how you, personally, can help transform your team.

SECTION FOUR
The Me

SECTION FOUR
OVERVIEW

Why ME? The beauty of focusing on the ME is that you become fully alive and engaged. When you show up real, open, and honest as a whole person—not just in the safety of your role—your energy inspires your team. You build loyalty and engagement on the team and become a lightning rod for others to bring more of themselves to the game. People want to feel comfortable enough to share their true opinions, feelings, and desires—to show up real.

Being real will create more conflict, both inside you and within the team, because more information, ideas, and opinions come to the table. But as we've demonstrated, you want this conflict because the expansion of new views and passion is the raw material and juice that drives creativity on your team. (Don't worry, we'll tell you how to work with those different opinions in the next section: 'The WE.')

The ME is about being aware of, and taking responsibility for, what is happening inside of you. This goes for the rest of the people on your team as well. And it is about developing the skills to work with your internal landscape.

A common myth says it is better to show up at work, do your job, and then be a real person at home. We disagree. Doing so is compartmentalization, which is ultimately harmful to the mind, body, emotions, and spirit of every person who makes that choice.

While compartmentalizing is human, leaders sometimes take it to the extreme, becoming so focused on their goals that they treat themselves and others around them like objects rather than people. People are not machines. You and your colleagues are living, breathing, creative organisms. You have hearts, minds, souls, and bodies. Stop acting as if you don't!

In this section, we'll give you the concepts, practical tools, and tips to handle yourself in those tough oh, sh*t! moments and help transform your team that is either stuck in or avoiding conflict. Do you want to be the type of leader who turns a team from stalled, dysfunctional, and unproductive into one that is innovative, productive, and has a competitive advantage? Read on!

CHAPTER 10
Power or Strength: Which is More Effective?

Meet Jake. He's a big guy at six-feet, five-inches. When he walks into a room, he dominates the crowd.

Since the beginning of his career, Jake has been a success. He quickly climbed the corporate ladder, effortlessly taking each rung, rising to the very top of his company by his late thirties. He knew how to control a situation and juggle anything tossed his way. Jake was a doer who made things happen. He controlled situations, drove events, and crossed the finish line first. He was a hero.

Once at the top, though, Jake discovered that his leadership style was no longer effective. He couldn't control people the way he had controlled situations or tasks. The problem: he focused on his own productivity rather than connecting, influencing, and working through others. Enter vulnerability.

If control is on one end of the spectrum, vulnerability is on the other. Vulnerability was something Jake stayed far, far away from. When we met Jake, he faced the formidable challenge of developing the next generation of leaders. That's hard to do without becoming fully alive and engaged; that is, considering the ME.

As executive coaches, we see many leaders like Jake who have experienced nothing but success, and then suddenly bump into a conundrum. These leaders know all about power and control. They don't consider that vulnerability or self-revelation is part of the solution.

POWER, MEET STRENGTH

During our first session with Jake, we introduced him to our Power and Strength Continuum model (see below). Fluid movement along this continuum is key to successful navigation between managing (getting control of a situation or people) and leading (connecting and influencing people).

THE POWER AND STRENGTH CONTINUUM[4]

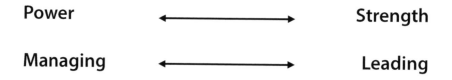

Our culture teaches us that when we win an authority figure's approval, we gain a certain level of power and control. Babies quickly learn that if they cry, someone will pick them up or feed them. Basic cause and effect. Children learn that when they get good grades or win the game, they get approval. They learn that they receive praise for having the right answer, and that being right is much better received than revealing that you don't understand.

As adults seeking power or control at work, we may do whatever it takes to win and not let anyone know when we are uncertain or don't have an answer. At home, we try to be the best or perfect parent by becoming the little league coach or heading up the school fundraiser. Though getting good grades and being the perfect parent are admirable endeavors, often the motivation is applause, approval, or acceptance. We want to feed our *ideal* status. Unfortunately, we lose connection with our authentic selves in the process.

Children learn to use power as an antidote to uncertainty and a sense of helplessness as they grow. To dominate and control the world around them is a viable solution to uncertainty and the unknown. The alternative solution, although not as popular, is strength: the capacity to accept oneself and turn inward, listen to yourself, and make decisions based on inner guidance, your gut instincts, rather than what others want or expect. However, this alternative involves embracing uncertainty and acknowledging that there is and will always be an unknown.

It stands to reason that most individuals believe it's better to control themselves and the environment than to feel the vulnerability and uncertainty of living in the unknown or a world without a *right* answer. We reinforce this belief when we continue to resolve feelings of uncertainty and helplessness by acquiring more power and control.

THE POWER AND STRENGTH CONTINUUM[5]

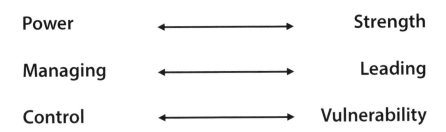

Power	←——→	Strength
Managing	←——→	Leading
Control	←——→	Vulnerability

In fact, most people find it easier and easier to objectify themselves and others—depersonalizing, treating people as objects, and keeping the world at a distance. The alternative, on the other end of the continuum, is to be personal—reveal ourselves in the moment and accept the world as it is presented. This latter option moves further and further into the background the more a person uses power and control.

THE POWER AND STRENGTH CONTINUUM[6]

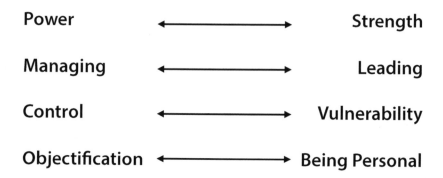

Power	⟷	Strength
Managing	⟷	Leading
Control	⟷	Vulnerability
Objectification	⟷	Being Personal

From the power and control side of the continuum comes a great deal of external success and achievement. Creating specific outcomes and being rewarded externally comes with significant applause. If you work hard, you get the raise, the promotion, the big title. You become the high performer in the organization. Who can resist those rewards? People are wired to want approval. It's natural that we strive for accolades and advancement, but that gets us stuck on the wrong side of the continuum.

The alternative to achievement is mastery (see below). That's a big statement, we know. Hang with us while we explain.

Mastery is not fixed to a particular external outcome, but rather to a growing internal sense of competence and satisfaction. This internal sense of competence and satisfaction also comes with achievement; however, it is not the critical measure of achievement. We tend to measure achievement by external signs of success. Mastery can be elusive for someone who has been heavily rewarded externally for achievements. The problem for high achievers and those who rest solidly on the power/control side of the continuum is they typically only know they are *good enough* when they hear applause or meet the expectations of others or of society.

THE POWER AND STRENGTH CONTINUUM[7]

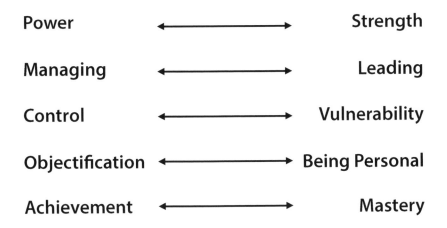

Power	← →	Strength
Managing	← →	Leading
Control	← →	Vulnerability
Objectification	← →	Being Personal
Achievement	← →	Mastery

Jake was very successful operating on the power side of the equation. However, there are two reasons it is important for leaders like Jake to reconnect to their ME and include the strength side of the equation.

The first reason is simple. As leaders rise to the top of an organization, they enter a fishbowl, with people watching everything they do. In other words, they become vulnerable and exposed to potential harm. From this place, a leader can choose either to be reactive and scramble to increase power and control, or to be responsive and bring forward more of himself in order to be more human.

For someone like Jake, being real, open, and honest is counterintuitive because his success has come through power and control.

The second reason leaders should reconnect to their ME is that it is the most effective way to influence people. Leaders who are real enough to reveal themselves earn more loyalty and engagement from the people on their team. They create an opening for connection that doesn't exist from the power/control side of the continuum.

We had many discussions with Jake about this Power and Strength Continuum. Jake would go away and chew on it, and he always came back with a reason to stay in control. That was until one day when he came in, plopped down in the chair across from us, and let out a big sigh.

"I just don't know how to do this," he said. "I don't know where to begin. I don't even know what my strengths are!"

We told him that, in that moment, he had made the first step toward vulnerability. From then on, Jake was completely different in our sessions. He applied his drive and energy to developing new ME muscles: revealing himself, being personal, and sharing both his strengths and weaknesses.

A couple of months later, we facilitated a strategy session with his team. We kicked off the day with some ME work, discussing styles. Rather than standing up and commanding the room like he normally did, Jake sat back and said, "I have to admit, while I have been a great doer, I haven't cracked the code of how to be a great leader. I've made some mistakes with you guys."

At first his team argued with him, apparently uncomfortable with his realness. "No way, Jake," they said. "We think you're great."

Jake responded, "Hey, thanks for the vote of confidence, but I know I need to improve in some areas, and I need feedback from you guys if I am going to get better."

For the rest of the day his team relaxed and, indeed, even spoke up to offer Jake some constructive feedback. One team member said, "I appreciated when you handed me the project, but then when we hit one delay you took over. I never got it back, which didn't help my project management confidence."

Jake responded, "I can see your point. I didn't even think about the impact on you."

We worked with Jake and his team for several months after that, and Jake brought more and more of himself to his work. At the end of our coaching relationship, Jake could move flexibly between power and strength. The intention was never for him to shift permanently to the strength and vulnerability side of the continuum. Ideally, a leader moves fluidly between the two sides of the continuum as appropriate for the situation.

Strength and vulnerability are not always the right answer. There are situations when you definitely want power and control. For example, in a crisis, a leader's ability to take charge, make clear decisions, and give direct orders creates a calm atmosphere and success. The key is to know you have a choice, and to develop your ME muscles to make that choice.

Don't be stuck on the power side of the continuum, or the strength side for that matter. An effective leader (and person) has the awareness, flexibility, and willingness to move from power to strength and back again, rather than planting themselves firmly on either end of the continuum.

A year later, Jake called us in again. He was now in charge of leadership development across the entire organization and invited us to partner with him to develop and conduct their intensive leadership development training sessions.

At the first session we could hardly believe our eyes and ears. There stood Big Jake in the front of seventy-five people, kicking off the training by talking about the importance of being vulnerable, self-revealing, and sharing weaknesses and strengths. He opened up about his own struggles with these concepts and the journey we had taken together. Everyone listened in rapt attention.

We knew our work that day would be easy. Leaders have amazing influence when they let down their walls, reveal themselves, and connect. Exercising those vulnerability muscles develops the ME and creates a high fidelity that influences others. People trust people who are real.

Do you know how to be a high-performing leader? Read on.

CHAPTER 11
Tempering Anger Doesn't Work

Do you think of yourself as a high-performing leader? If not, do you want to become one?

Leadership isn't confined to a specific role or position, although that fits. We define leadership as *the level of influence you have* from any role in the organization. Leadership has much more to do with embodiment than it does with titles or positions bestowed by someone from the outside. True leadership comes from the inside out.

Leadership surfaces when you are solid inside yourself—you know what you think, feel, and want. You express it through willingness and ability to influence, and to be influenced by, the people around you and the circumstances you're in.

A good leader masters the movement along two key axes:

- The ME—the space within yourself
- The WE—the space between you and others

We focus in this section on the ME; we'll get to the WE in the next section.

Most leaders we work with want to increase their influence and effectiveness. When we ask them what they're doing to reach their goal, they tell us about the conferences they attend, the business books they read, and the podcasts they listen to. They ask for input from their peers and bosses, and they attempt to follow the latest success formulas.

Sound reasonable? Something critical is missing.

Leaders tend to focus on external input and applying tips, tools, and formulas to drive great results. That makes for a fantastic résumé with terrific achievements. These endeavors may even impress all the right people.

While this achievement mentality works for a while, an outside-in leadership development approach is ultimately not sustainable. Eventually, you'll need to turn inward to understand how you operate, know when you tend to react defensively versus respond productively, and learn to ride the waves of the fluctuating human emotions. Turning inward develops self-mastery, and it may be the number one biggest lever for increasing your leadership influence, as well as your team's and organization's creativity and effectiveness.

INSIDE-OUT FOCUS

Self-mastery requires an inside-out leadership focus, beginning with self-discovery: what is going on inside of you? Self-mastery entails learning how to operate this human called *you*. From there you can learn to work with and master the fluctuations that occur in your own internal environment.

Most of us are wired to look outside ourselves to determine if we are doing okay. But this view is warped, because our *compare and contrast* equation has very little to do with what is happening inside other people. There is a common saying, *Don't compare your inside to someone else's outside.* When you do, you only see one side of the story.

Like other leaders, you may judge yourself from the outside first, meaning you're okay if everyone around you is happy, or if you win, get the promotion, or complete all your work. Now, don't get us wrong. Of course, you want those things to happen. The problem comes when you make those outside things *more important* than what is going on inside. That moves you to try to change, construct, or manage yourself to please others and meet their expectations rather than make yourself happy.

This outside-first approach develops what we call a *siloed* person. A siloed person's life is compartmentalized. She manages her behavior for effect and treats herself and others like objects to be manipulated instead of as complex, emotional beings to be heard and considered. When things don't work out well, she doubles down and works even harder to look good, be in control, and shape herself into trendy styles and forms that are the latest, greatest examples of high performance.

When you try to meet those outside expectations, you repress your natural human tendencies and compress your own energy, which is why this behavior doesn't work for long. Eventually, you need to release this natural energy inside of you. If you've repressed it for some time, it likely emerges as an explosion, a failure, or an emotional or physical breakdown.

Rather than focus outside, your task as a leader is to be aware of what is going on inside yourself. Inside-out focus enables you to identify what you are thinking, feeling, and wanting in any given moment.

It sounds simple. But do you easily recognize what's going on inside you? When something new is happening for you, do you recognize:

- Your thoughts: How does the new information bump against your own belief system?
- Your feelings: What is happening in your body physiologically? When you connect to your physical body and simplify what is going on inside, you'll notice that you are either opening or closing, leaning forward or leaning away, feeling close to or

distant from another person, idea, or situation. Explore and identify what you feel inside.

- Your intentions: Do you know what you really want in this situation? For example, do you want to convince the other person and get your way? Do you want to understand the other person's point of view? Or, are you interested in repairing the connection between you? Check in with yourself and notice.

Too often, inner awareness does not come until our insides are screaming, at which point *management* is required to avoid eruption or implosion!

SURF THE WAVES

Self-mastery is like surfing. On a surfboard, it's critical to notice the water's rhythm, see the wave rising, anticipate the wave's size, and time your decision based upon a solid ability to work with the water's movement so you can ride the wave. Surfing requires self-mastery. It's not about having the perfect high-end surfboard. And it's certainly not about the impossible feat of controlling the water—good luck with that! Surfing is about mastering the relationship between you, the board, and the water.

In the same way, leadership is not about having a stellar résumé or multiple accolades. We can't control our humanness; that's even trickier to tame than a wave. But we can master the relationship between our inner self and the world in which we live and work.

Leaders often make the mistake of focusing on *a better surfboard,* or hell, upgrading to a boat! They construct themselves from the outside in to stay afloat through a storm or ride through rough water. The better the boat looks, the more they assume it is water-ready and safe.

Sadly, when leaders look outward, they miss the real opportunity to create a relationship with their inner emotional world. They don't learn to ride the ebb and flow of strong emotional waves.

Self-mastery entails integrating new information and understanding what fits for you and what doesn't. You ride the wave with the surfboard you have, and that tool becomes an extension of your body. When you have self-mastery, you can pause and turn inward to be aware of the waves *inside of you*. Instead of reacting to the waves, you embrace them, you lean into them like a horse leans in to an attacker. When you lean in, you more easily digest what you learn, keep what fits, and throw out what doesn't.

THE FIRST STEP TO SELF-MASTERY

Self-mastery begins with gathering information about yourself. Be aware of what is happening inside of you. What thought patterns come up for you repeatedly? What physical sensations do you notice? What emotional tones occur? Finally, do you notice your intuitive hunches?

Self-mastery requires turning up the volume of what is happening inside of you and gathering this information over time. We offer a tool to help you do that the *Three-Point Check*, which is to be used in conjunction with *Interested Curiosity*.

Tool: Three-Point Check

The Three-Point Check involves pausing at least three times a day to notice:

- What am I thinking?
- What am I feeling?
- What do I want right now?

Capture your findings on a notepad. Do this for a week and review your notes. What patterns do you find? As you review your findings, engage the next important quality, interested curiosity.

Interested Curiosity

Rather than label what you notice as right or wrong, consider that the thought, feeling, or intention is there for *good reason*. It might be an outdated reason. Something you learned growing up was probably helpful when you learned it, but maybe it no longer serves you.

Approach whatever you notice with interested curiosity. Ask yourself, "I wonder what's driving my thought, feeling, and intention in this situation?"

This exercise helps you uncover more about yourself instead of *getting rid* of something you deem unattractive. Despite our best efforts, we don't change by making ourselves wrong. We change when we are curious about, learn what's underneath, and understand the problem that the thought, feeling, or intention is trying to solve. This exercise of curiosity is often enough for our so-called *negative* patterns to dissipate. If you want to apply these tools for yourself, download *The Oh Sh*t! Kit* at www.Thriveinc.com/beautyofconflict/bonus.

See how our past client Charlie got great value from the *Three-Point Check* using interested curiosity.

CHARLIE EMBRACES HIS ANGER

Charlie was an up-and-coming executive in a fast-growing technology company struggling with a series of angry explosions at work. His superiors told him his advancement would be limited, as would his career at the company, if he didn't stop reacting so unproductively.

Charlie attended an anger management class on company recommendation. He learned the importance of shutting down his anger and communicating in a more respectful style when he was upset. It helped for a while. That is, until about two months after the class, when Charlie blew up again. Repressing his angry feelings wasn't going so well.

When we try to *get rid of* or suppress our emotions, they go underground in our bodies only to pop out unproductively somewhere else, like with other people. They may even show up as physical symptoms. We have emotional energy for good reason. Knowing what drives it is the key to unraveling the pattern.

A few months later, we met Charlie in person at one of our six-month leadership-development programs. We conducted an in-person module shortly after the start of the program. Charlie traveled from China to Montana to attend. His goal: to get rid of his anger.

We emphasized the importance of understanding, owning, and acknowledging *unpopular* feelings such as anger, rage, and frustration. We also explored why it's unhealthy to shut down these feelings or to get rid of them. Charlie was surprised by the discussion. He assumed the different approaches to anger reflected a cultural difference between China and the US. We quickly explained that American executives are also trained and encouraged to control, manage, and get rid of negative feelings. We just don't agree that the approach is effective.

We encouraged Charlie to be curious about his anger, rage, and righteousness by asking himself, "What is driving my anger in this situation?" We suggested that he get to know, understand, and fully acknowledge that part of himself with curiosity. This would give him a choice when those strong *negative* emotions began to surface.

Charlie was intrigued. Even better, he was willing to give it a try.

Throughout our work together, both in-person and virtually in the months following, Charlie got over the belief that he had to get rid of his anger. Once he accepted that his anger was natural, he started to make progress. In fact, it gave him vital information about what wasn't working for him.

First, he did the *Three-Point Check* three times a day. He became aware of triggers and patterns both inside and outside that escalated his anger. He noticed two triggers and came up with ways to work with them.

Charlie's first trigger was poor performance. When someone gave Charlie a project that clearly missed the mark, he got riled up. Because he was working on self-mastery, rather than resort to exploding, he now paused to do a full Three-Point Check:

- Thinking: This person is incompetent!
- Feeling: That's easy—rage!
- Wanting: People to do what I tell them to do!

This *Three-Point Check* gave him some space to consider with interested curiosity: What's driving my reaction? He realized that he didn't think people were hearing him. As a result, he shifted his approach. Instead of yelling, he would ask his team member, "What did you understand the assignment was about?"

More than once, the person related something that was clearly not what Charlie had wanted. Each time, Charlie was surprised. He became even more curious, asking, "Wow! How did we get so far apart?"

Again, more than one person said, "I don't always understand what you want me to do. I don't ask questions because I don't want you to get angry."

This information helped Charlie improve the way he gave assignments. He spent more time getting people on the same page, and he was much happier with the results.

Charlie's second trigger was hunger. He realized that he was more apt to get upset around 4 p.m. His *Three-Point Check* revealed the relationship between his hunger and his anger. He incorporated a 3:30 p.m. protein bar to his routine, and everyone was happier.

Even if you do not have an anger issue like Charlie, you can still increase your leadership influence and effectiveness through self-mastery, the inside-out leadership development approach. Self-mastery is about knowing and owning one's inner landscape as much, or even more than, focusing on meeting others' expectations. Trainings, conferences, and business gurus are all helpful, but don't stop there.

Use the *Three-Point Check* to understand what you think, feel, and want at any given moment. Want support practicing, download *The Oh Sh*t! Kit* at www.Thriveinc.com/beautyofconflict/bonus.

The information you gather will give you valuable insight. Then, approach what you notice with interested curiosity. Ask yourself what's driving this thought, feeling, and intention so you can get underneath the pattern and unravel it. This is where the surfboard meets the water!

Let's move from the surfboard to the pasture. Because, as we've already discussed, horses have a lot to teach us, especially when it comes to the ME.

CHAPTER 12
Horses and Leadership

Horses teach leaders more in one day than most training programs teach in a year. A good number of successful leaders in history were good with horses as well as with people: Alexander the Great, Katherine the Great, George Washington, Winston Churchill, and Ronald Reagan,[8] to name a few.

We saw earlier how horses are masters at picking up clues and reading their environment. Horses thrive in herds, where they regularly relate to and communicate with each other. They set boundaries and manage various interactions while paying remarkable attention to everything going on around them.

Horses are emotional intelligence experts. Their expertise stems from their need to recognize danger and respond in the moment. They are excellent teachers and mirrors for us humans. If you can successfully lead a horse, you are likely effective with people. Working with a horse forces you to develop your ME, because leading a horse requires getting in touch with what's going on inside of you.

Put a leader in a round pen with a horse, and the horse will quickly become a crystal clear mirror for that leader's congruence in building a relationship and giving instructions. Horses teach the power of pause. Let's look at two stories that illustrate just how powerfully our four-legged friends can impact leadership.

INSIDE-OUT AND CONGRUENT LEADERSHIP

I, Susan, learned about leading from the inside out during a workshop run by Koelle Simpson at a ranch in Phoenix in 2011. The workshop focused on learning about leadership from horses.

The only problem: I was not a horse person. I loved watching them from afar, but I was not one to get too close.

Even so, on day one, I was the first person to volunteer to walk into the round pen with a horse and see what happened. The general instruction was simply to establish a relationship with the horse. Easy enough, right?

Some details. The round pen is a circular enclosure about fifty feet in diameter. You walk in the round pen with no equipment. The horse has no halter, you have no rope. It is just you and the horse in an enclosed round pen.

There I sat with fifteen other participants in the bleacher-like seats above the round pen. Although I enthusiastically stood up, I immediately had second thoughts as I made my way down to the ground. My doubts grew stronger as I approached the round pen entrance and heard the sounds of the horse that was inside.

Inside, I panicked. But, I wasn't about to look scared or chicken out. It was time to muster up some courage and walk in that round-pen door. So, I did what any good leader does under pressure: I put on a happy, confident face and walked right in.

That horse stayed as far away from me as possible. I tried looking calm and cool. I tried moving toward the horse, following all of the recommended tips: eyes down, curved movements, nonaggressive posture, visualizing the horse letting me get closer.

I got nothing. As I stood near the center of the pen, the horse was restless and stayed against the wall twenty-five feet away from me.

Koelle coached me. "What's going on inside?" she asked me. "What are you thinking and feeling? What is your intention in connecting with the horse?"

After some feeble attempts to answer intelligently, I broke down. "Honestly, I'm scared silly of this horse," I said, looking at Koelle. I was almost in tears, hating myself for jumping into the pen first. "I have no idea what I'm doing, and frankly, I'm not even sure I'd be comfortable if that horse got any closer."

I heard muttering from the others watching. I wrestled with my tears. Finally, I lost the battle and let a few run down my cheek.

Suddenly, I felt the breath of the horse on my neck. Wow, I did not see that coming! Unbeknownst to me, the horse began moving closer the moment I was honest and congruent about what was happening for me.

I knew I wanted to jump in and get the most out of the workshop, but what I wasn't willing to acknowledge or own was my fear of the horse. I wanted to learn from the horse, but I didn't want to look scared. The horse figured that out in seconds. It took me a while longer!

Leaders often find it necessary to step up and take charge of a situation. I tried to do that with the horse with my faux confidence. But if, when you take charge, you deny your inner fear or doubts, you will be less effective at leading, just as I initially failed to win over the horse.

Horses taught me that if I acknowledge, even to myself, my nervousness around these powerful animals, and I take a breath to be present with that nervousness and excitement, I settle down. Connecting to the

ME clarifies what direction to go next. And the horse doesn't seem to mind at all.

The same applies to leading people. When a leader acknowledges her feelings; be it fear, excitement, joy, sorrow, or hurt, leadership is easier. Often, just acknowledging your emotions to yourself can be powerful. When you become aware of and own your thoughts, feelings, and wants, you clarify the fidelity of your message because there is congruence between the external words being spoken and the internal emotional landscape. Individuals feel safe in that congruence just as horses do; and, people tend to be loyal to congruent leaders.

Over the next couple of days, I experienced the amazing power of horses as mirrors. The experience was so profound that I signed up for Koelle's year-long Equus Coaching Program. I now regularly use horses in my work with leaders and teams, which is easy to do here in the horse country of Montana. It is powerful to work with a business leader who suddenly finds true leadership in a round pen with a horse. Leaders develop a felt sense they can rely on when leading their teams.

Next up: the power of pause. Yes, we'll learn that from a horse, too.

THE POWER OF PAUSE

It's easy for leaders to focus on the vision, goal, or milestones. Yet this emphasis often comes at the expense of noticing what is happening inside. When we lose our connection to self, we lose our connection to others. As a result, we don't realize how our actions impact our colleagues and team. Our best plans and approaches are counterproductive.

Years after my own round pen experience, I (Susan) coached Bridgette, a senior manager for a technology company. Bridgette struggled on a project in which she was partnering with her boss. It was not going smoothly.

I opted to use a round pen in my coaching. For Bridgette that meant a session involving a horse with a halter and Bridgette holding the end-lead line connected to the horse. This connection to the horse via the lead line helps the leader (in this case, Bridgette) recognize that her internal feelings are transmitted via the line to the horse (who is a stand-in for the team). For example, when Bridgette is tense, her grip tightens. The horse feels this tension and reacts. I've found this type of coaching to be the quickest way for a leader to get a sense of her leadership communication, impact, and effectiveness.

As Bridgette interacted with the horse, the horse crowded her. Bridgette stiffened her body, hunched her shoulders up to her ears, and she could hardly breathe. First, I suggested she take a breath and feel her feet. Bridgette chuckled because she didn't realize she had been holding in her breath. Her energy shifted, and she looked more relaxed.

Second, I suggested she let the horse know what a comfortable distance would be, meaning set a boundary by turning toward the horse and using her energy and her body to back the horse out of her space. Because Bridgette was now more grounded in her body, she could use the lead line to effectively communicate her physical space boundary. Success!

The next goal was to partner with the horse to create movement, much like a dance, moving the horse forward and back. Holding the lead line and facing the horse, but to the side of its head, Bridgette stepped forward toward the tail of the horse. The horse backed up. Bridgette stepped backward, and the horse came toward her. She played around with this movement, and each time the horse responded immediately.

Finally, I suggested she lead the horse by shifting speeds, and communicate the desired goal and when to stop. I watched her attempts.

What was most interesting, and illustrative to Bridgette's current work situation, came up as she led the horse. It didn't go well. Bridgette would start with a clear goal in mind. She looked serious and would stride ahead with purpose, and as she moved, the horse would begin to move. But, at some point it pulled backward against her with increasing pressure. Bridgette did manage to bring the horse along, but the task was exhausting!

I stepped in and modeled what I had seen her do with the horse. Watching, Bridgette said, "I see what I'm doing. I'm so focused on getting to my goal that I'm dragging the horse along."

"Yes," I replied. "My story is that in your goal-focused mind you've lost contact with your own body and, as a result, with the horse. You can't expect to move a 1,500-pound animal if you don't even inhabit your own 150-pound body."

I suggested she pause during the process to connect to herself first. Bridgette paused. She took a breath, felt her feet, and grounded into her whole body. The horse visibly relaxed, and when Bridgette again attempted to lead the horse, he easily followed.

Bridgette recognized the impact of focusing only on her goal, and she discovered the power of pausing and connecting to herself before simply pushing on—or, in this case, pulling or dragging. This simple session made a profound shift for Bridgette. She recognized that at work she was so focused on the goal of a project—driving for the deadline—that she missed the connection to herself and her boss. No wonder he kept resisting her ideas!

In life and in leadership, it is easy to focus on the vision, goal, or milestones. But this emphasis comes at the expense of noticing what is happening internally. When you lose connection with yourself, you lose connection to others and miss out on the impact you can have on them.

Have you, like Bridgette, ever been too focused on driving your own agenda? Have you ever been like me; so overcome by what you feel that you're not being congruent? Focusing on a goal is not a bad thing. The key is to remember yourself in the midst of achieving that goal, and to be aware of the larger arena or context you are operating within. When you include the entire landscape, both inside and out, you'll be surprised how graceful and easy it is to accomplish that goal you have been striving for so hard. When you pause, when you become congruent, when you connect to your ME, your leadership improves.

Have you ever felt better when you blamed someone else for a problem? I know I have. But playing the blame game undermines your influence. Read on to find out how, and what you can do about it.

CHAPTER 13
Why Blame Backfires

You are always creating your own reality. We all are. When you find yourself in conflict, your great brain floods with emotion and loses its rational capacity. That doesn't feel good. As a result, the reality you create gets skewed.

In fact if you are like most people, you tend to believe conflict is being done *to you* rather than *by you*. The villains are out there, and you are the hapless victim.

This perspective creates distance between people and their own involvement. They play the blame game to make themselves feel better and defuse inner tension.

We know you are more sophisticated than that. But take a moment to remember the last time you got into a significant disagreement at work. Did you rationalize your behavior, even to yourself? Maybe you even used that classic line: *It's not personal. It's just business.*

Now think about a time with your spouse, or even better, your teenage child, doing just what you asked them not to do. Wasn't their behavior simply out of line? Or wrong? And now you can't play the not personal/

just business card, can you? It's very personal, and it feels like they did it just to make you mad!

When you as a leader take the point of view that conflict happens without your full participation—meaning it's not personal—you reduce your influence and effectiveness, especially in the midst of conflict. Luckily, the reverse is also true: when you opt in and take responsibility for your part in creating the conflict, you have the power to change your response. By understanding the ME, you can influence the outcome more productively and creatively.

INFORMATION TECHNOLOGY AND ME

We committed to a year-long engagement with an information technology consulting firm. We had the role of leadership team advisors. Henry, the CEO and managing partner, had worked with us at a previous company and wanted support getting his new team up to speed.

At the three-month mark, we arrived onsite to facilitate a strategy meeting. The team talked about a recent problem with closing new clients. The cause of the slow-close rate came up in discussion.

Jessica, head of Business Development, piped up with full force, "Well, that's easy. Rob, you're too anal! These are simple proposals. We just need a two-page discussion document. You're taking forever and making them way too long. I can't close clients with that!"

"Really?" Rob retorted. "You're saying my work is too detailed?"

"Don't take it so personally," Jessica shot back. "I just don't need a thirty-page white paper. I need something to let them know we can understand their pain and know how to help them."

You might be thinking Jessica's point is logical and valid. Logical, yes. Data-driven, maybe. Influential? We're not so sure.

The biggest issue was that Jessica fell into the classic blame game. It's not uncommon. Blaming others means you don't have to acknowledge your part in the problem (and you do, by the way, have a part in the problem).

What's missing is self-responsibility. It's a ME part of the equation.

We define self-responsibility as taking responsibility for creating your own experience or acknowledging how you have contributed to the problem. This might be as simple as an unhelpful reaction.

The concept of self-responsibility, and the idea that we create our own experiences, can be hard to swallow. On the reverse, we easily assimilate concepts like *It's not personal. It's just business.* But that point of view creates distance between the event and our own involvement.

Is it really just business? All our clients seem to take their work quite personally. They commit their time, energy, heartbeats, and passion to what they do throughout each day. How is that not personal?

Viktor Frankl, author of *Man's Search for Meaning*, took charge of his experience while locked in a German concentration camp for Jews. He wrote, "Between stimulus and response, there is a space. In that space is our power to choose our response. In our response lies our growth and our freedom."

Often, the stimulus evokes a feeling so strong that we override or separate from that emotional response through a rational reaction. By more fully developing emotional intelligence and allowing for the feeling, we are more apt to respond, and not simply react!

We bypass the choice point when we go immediately to blame. In so doing, we give away our power.

There are probably times you do a good job of pretending not to feel anything in the midst of conflict. That convinces you that you're not responsible for the problem. That distance from your genuine thoughts, feelings, and intentions, however, creates the biggest problem. When you get too far from yourself—when you forget the ME—it's easy to forget that you are a player and that you create your experience and impact others' experiences. You also can easily deny that you care about the impact you have on those around you. This pretense leads to inhuman responses that don't help resolve conflict.

GETTING PERSONAL: WHAT TO ASK

You impact your world at home, at work, and heck, even while commuting. Ask yourself these questions in the midst of conflict to better understand your impact and to avoid blaming others for your situation:

- How much am I influencing the situation?
- What responsibility am I willing to take for my impact?
- Am I up to the challenge of owning what I create: the good, the bad, the ugly, and the beautiful?

Truth be told, it takes tremendous courage to say yes to the last question. *It's not personal. It's just business* is way easier. But that's the coward's way out. Are you up for the challenge?

Taking responsibility means owning what you create. When you're at odds with someone else, take responsibility by:

- Turning inside yourself and being aware of what you think, feel, and want. It may take you some time to get through your automatic defenses. Slow down, take a breath, and really sense what is happening for you.
- Determining what to bring back out. Choose what you will say and do to take responsibility for the situation in order to make a positive influential impact.

- Taking responsibility for what is happening inside of you. Blame blocks energy. Your openness will foster amazing, creative solutions.

Let's go back to Jessica. She started with direct blame: "Rob, you're too anal! These are simple proposals."

Points for Jessica: at least she is communicating directly to Rob (albeit in a blame-y way), rather than having hushed conversations about Rob with a coworker. "Rob is so anal. He can't put a simple proposal together!" We call this *gossip blame*. It completely undermines team trust and is toxic for the company overall.

CrisMarie jumped in, "We appreciate your viewpoint Jessica, but you seem to have decided you're right and Rob is wrong. I'm curious what happens (inside) for you regarding these proposals?"

Jessica slowed down, turned inside to the ME, and noticed what she was thinking, feeling, and wanting. "I realize I feel stressed trying to walk potential clients through such a detailed proposal. I am relationship-based. I suck at the details. Plus, I haven't closed a single client. So I'm not feeling so great about my results. I know I am good at what I do. I want to get my sales success back!"

With this clarity, Jessica was able to see her role in the situation. She now had more influential input than when she pointed her finger and complained about Rob.

She said to Rob, "I'm uncomfortable with how long your proposal documents are, and I'm the one that has to walk the potential client through them. I really want to have something simple that I can use and be successful with so I can win some business."

As a result of this interchange, Rob and Jessica collaborated to create a solution that worked for both of them. They designed a five-page slide deck that could be easily customized for different clients and worked great with Jessica's conversational style with clients. They closed more clients, made more money, and felt successful!

BREAKING THROUGH TO CREATIVITY

It is easy to assume someone else is to blame for conflict and miss that you are always creating your own experience. It's easy to fall back to: *It's not personal. It's just business.* But when you do, you miss out on taking self-responsibility, showing up authentically, and influencing with a creative solution.

Rather than focus on what Rob was or was not doing to make her world miserable, Jessica had to own her discomfort and be explicit about her style and her burning desire to be successful. Taking responsibility empowered her to make a different choice—to influence Rob. Even though Rob is more detail oriented and takes more time developing proposals than Jessica likes, everything is on the table now, and there is more room for creativity.

Bottom line: you can't change the Robs on your team, but you can have powerful influence by saying what is happening inside of you rather than blaming others. Do that, and watch the energy and innovation increase on your team.

Next, we'll show you what to do with emotions (e-gads!) at work.

CHAPTER 14
Why You Should Be Emotional at Work

Business carries a tacit, maybe even explicit, rule that emotions and emotional expression are not okay. People who *get emotional* are seen as weak, defective, or unprofessional. Emotions are inefficient and will take you off course from your work. Basically, feelings are bad, and people who express them are dismissed.

In spite of our discomfort with emotional expression in ourselves or others, our emotions are a key linkage to our ME.

Emotional energy can be hard to bear. A coworker who breaks down in tears at the conference table or a boss who vents his anger can cause shock and discomfort. But we believe emotions are the key that accesses intuition and creativity. Emotions help us create better connections and relationships.

The problem is most people haven't been trained to work with emotions—their own or other people's. Do you relate? If so, maybe you tend to suppress or repress how you feel, or maybe you ignore or shut down others' emotional reactions. When you stifle feelings, you limit access to valuable energy and information that could guide you to better decision making, creativity, and connection.

Actually, it makes perfect sense that people *get emotional* at work as they bump into obstacles and challenges to move a project forward. When smart, passionate people rally around an inspiring goal, their emotional energy can move the project forward. You want their passion (emotions), you want their inspiration (emotions), and yes, you want their smarts (different opinions).

People tend to be okay with positive emotions, but not okay with negative ones such as sadness and anger. I, CrisMarie, am no exception. I've had to learn to welcome my own messy emotions.

CRISMARIE'S EMOTIONAL OUTBURST

Several years ago, Susan and I led a monthly CEO group that had been through many years of ups and downs together. When a team member shared about his loss of a sibling when he was a young teen, immense sadness welled up in me.

I tried hard to swallow it down because I was embarrassed by my emotions in front of this group of mostly male leaders. I did not want to look weak by, heaven forbid, crying. But the energy in my body wouldn't obey, and I started to cry.

Not a soft, inconspicuous cry. I was loud, snotty, messy, sobbing. I was horrified.

I looked up through my tears to see more than one stunned face. Some people looked away uncomfortably. Others visibly braced against the onslaught of my emotional outburst. One guy asked with sarcasm: "Wow, do we need to take care of you?"

That stung, but it didn't take me out. I took a deep breath, gathered myself, and found my words. "No. I'm okay," I said. "I admit that surprised even me. What you don't know is that my brother died six months ago."

Silence filled the room. No more sarcastic comments or awkward shuffling.

I turned to the person who had shared about his sister dying. "I was touched by your story, and my own grief welled up inside of me," I told him. "Right now, I actually feel much more present and able to move forward." We carried on with the experience.

After our group dialogue, a healthy discussion ensued. Each person sitting around the table shared how he or she dealt with emotions on their teams.

One CEO had a female VP who reported to him. She was excellent at her job but seemed overly emotionally expressive. That meant lots of tears. He was so uncomfortable with her behavior that he was considering firing her. As a group, we talked about different ways to work with her.

Another CEO shared that in the start-up phase of his business, he had heart palpations. His doctor referred him to Susan as a business coach who suggested he do breath work for ten minutes a day. He hesitantly agreed to do this, but only behind his closed office door. While he breathed, he felt anger, and tears flowed from the pressure and responsibility he held. Within the first week of practicing deep breathing, he noticed a significant difference in his health, and his mental-emotional state allowed the anger and tears to flow. He continues to do breathing exercises to this day.

A third CEO, a woman, spoke about her own struggle to ensure she never cracked. She had learned early in her career that women in tears were doomed to a slow, flat career path. She found herself annoyed by emotionally expressive people, especially women. Paradoxically, she reported that earlier in her life, she was emotionally expressive and creative. Now her expression and creativity were restricted, and she especially missed feeling creative. After others spoke, she said, "Wow, I think my creativity has dimmed because of my restricted emotional expression."

This vulnerability and open conversation shifted the energy in the room. Though we had to shorten our regular agenda, that session was one of the most mentioned, and also was voted as the most valuable over other topics. It wouldn't have happened at all had I not been surprised by my own emotional, empathetic resonance.

OUT OF CONTROL AND INTO CREATIVITY

We can practically hear you thinking, "OMG! You're saying everyone should be processing all their emotions in the workplace! No way."

We agree. If excessive emotion like grief from the loss of a loved one surfaces, whoever is experiencing the emotions may benefit from professional emotional support. This is what CrisMarie did when she realized she was suppressing her grief after the loss of her brother.

However, people tend to be too black and white about the issue of emotions and can err on the side of stoicism. Emotions can make us feel out of control, so it makes sense to want to contain them.

Women especially take the hit for being *weak* or *too emotional.* But more and more research[9] shows that woman leaders are better at building relationships and demonstrating empathy. As a result, they are overall better at getting organizational results! Empathy is directly tied to our ability to resonate and feel emotion with another. Women do score higher on the *soft* skills, but in a Harvard Business Review study[10] that evaluated more than 7,200 people, women scored higher not only in the expected areas, but at every level! They were rated by their peers, bosses, direct reports, and their other associates as better leaders overall. This, we believe, speaks to the trust and influence that is built through empathetic relational leadership by men and women—our ability to feel and relate to the feelings of others.

Emotions are not a male or female thing. Emotional energy is a source of power all unto its own. Think about it. How often does creativity emerge in a measured, orderly way? More often it is a sense of loss of control that opens a mainline for creativity.

Creating a company culture where it is natural and normal to feel emotions (because it is) will allow you and your team to use this energy. It doesn't have to be complex or take lots of time.

A culture that is friendly to emotions creates space for you or someone else to share what is going on internally in the moment. It takes only about ninety seconds for someone to recognize their feelings. It takes longer for someone who is trying to avoid, explain, or make their reaction go away.

When someone is visibly upset, their thinking and attention suffers until they can process their feelings. This is not the time to continue discussing the content. Instead, check out what you as a leader notice.

For example, "Mary, it looks like you're upset about something. We value your input on this discussion, and I think you are preoccupied. I'm curious what is going on for you, and I'm willing to take a couple of minutes to talk about it."

If the person is not willing to share, don't push it. If they do want to speak, listen. Reflect back the gist of what you hear, both the content and the emotional tone. This acknowledges and validates them.

For example, "Sounds like you are frustrated that we didn't go with your original plan, and when Jamie brought up the same idea today, you think he's getting credit for your great idea. Does that fit?"

Allow the person to clarify whether or not you got their experience right.

Next, empathy helps when someone takes the risk to be honest. You can affirm without necessarily agreeing with the person.

For example, "No wonder you are so upset if you believe everyone thinks this is Jamie's great idea and not yours."

Finally, ask, "Is there something you need from me or from us to support you?" or "What can you do to support yourself in this situation?"

We won't lie, it can take some upfront time. But it saves wasted time and energy because it minimizes gossip, politics, and work delays when people feel comfortable to process their upsets real time.

Feeling emotions doesn't make you weak. Suppressing emotions doesn't make you strong. In fact, holding emotional energy inside actually drains mental and physical energy.

Emotional suppression also limits you to a one-dimensional perspective. The connection between mind and body (thinking and feeling) shows that allowing more emotional range and expression enhances quality of life, health, and happiness. Don't take our word for it. Check out the vast research in this area. To learn more, read the work by Bennett Wong and Jock McKeen, *Health & Happiness,* or Dr. Gabor Mate's *When the Body Says No.*

Emotional awareness and expression is critical to health and productivity. Feelings add heart and depth to individual experiences and allow access to intuition and creativity.

Do you want to feel intuitive and creative at work? Do you want to be influential? The next chapter tells you how.

CHAPTER 15
Two Characteristics of an Influential Leader

Want to be an influential leader? Then learn how to be both vulnerable and curious with yourself and your team. Vulnerability and curiosity are the two humanizing elements of leadership that increase your influence.

What gets in the way of being vulnerable and curious is when you treat yourself or others like a machine. Recognize you have a heart and a mind and be willing to connect to both. Tend to your ME before you attempt to lead others.

When you are vulnerable and acknowledge what you really think, feel, and want, your energy flows more fully. You have easier access to intuition and creativity. You are congruent with your words and actions, which match your intent. Humans pick up on that matching resonance, and it naturally engenders trust. Trust makes people willing, and often *wanting*, to follow you, the congruent leader.

Too often, leaders try to manage themselves. They've gone to well-meaning leadership schools and read books that advise them to compartmentalize themselves into different pieces: the leader and the person.

- The leader, or hero, who looks good, gets down to business, is result-driven, makes things happen, and lives by the adage: *Don't ever let them see you sweat!*

- The person, or human, who shows up in personal spheres with family, friends, and on social media.

We aren't big fans of the split between business and personal or the work leader and at-home person. Successful leaders are walking, talking models who embrace the fullness and challenges of being both the designated hero *and* the human being.

Isn't that really the challenge of a leader? The hero: taking the lead, confidently setting the course, inspiring others to follow, and making things happen. The human: staying aware of the vulnerability, uncertainty, and fears inherent in doing something new and risky. It's a tough balancing act.

Are you a hero, or simply human? You're both. So, what does it take to stay real and grounded when people look to you for so much more than that? What does it take to connect to the ME first?

Yes, we're going to talk about the two characteristics: vulnerability and curiosity again. But this time, we'll also address courage and show you how combining vulnerability and curiosity is the key to increasing your influence. Together, that's the stuff the ME is made of.

THE VULNERABLE, CURIOUS, COURAGEOUS ME

Vulnerability is the willingness to expose yourself to danger, to let others see you sweat, to acknowledge, "I don't know," "I made a mistake," or "I'm sorry."

We challenge you to risk baring your humanness when stepping into uncharted territory. That risk will take you miles in creating connection, influence, and loyalty. On the continuum of vulnerability, one end being hidden and the other end being real, strive to show up real.

ME AXIS

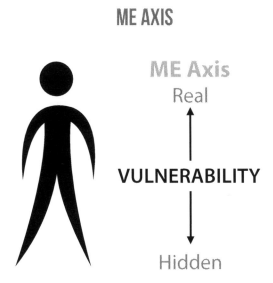

It's true that leaders need to have a strong opinion, confidence, and a vision for where to go. The more successful leader is also curious, interested, and actively seeking other ideas—a different perspective beyond his own experience and expertise.

We see curiosity as a continuum: closed or defended to the opinions of the other on one end; open-minded and willing to change point of view on the other.

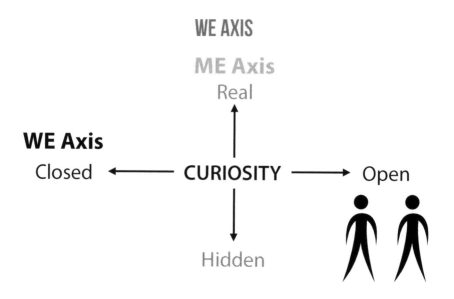

Even when you're convinced someone is completely wrong, muster up your willingness to be influenced and access your curiosity. First, focus on the ME by owning up to your own point of view: "Wow! I'm surprised. That is completely different from my perspective." Second, link to the WE and be curious: "Tell me how you came to your conclusion." Third, remain open to their logic. You may not agree, but the other's reasoning may still influence and change your final opinion or approach.

The irony is that being vulnerable (real and curious) and open to influence makes you most influential. That's because you are speaking up and revealing what you think, feel, and want while also considering the input of the other. This willingness and ability to open up while being real, while standing in the tension of differences is courageous and powerful. People connect to you and trust you, because you are real and open. You are an influencer.

MOST EFFECTIVE STYLES

ME Axis
Real

WE Axis
Closed ← → Open

Influencer

Hidden

A leader needs the courage to chart a new course, but now we are talking about a different type of courage. We mean the ability to tolerate the tension inherent in being a hero while also being curious and vulnerable, rather than making either the hero position or the human vulnerability right or wrong.

Tolerating tension takes courage. It requires handling failure and setbacks as well as acknowledging and owning your part in whatever the outcome. Courage means taking a moment to celebrate success, even knowing there is still a long road ahead. Yes, you still need to be a strong leader. Vulnerability and courage aren't about being weak. But too often leaders omit this softer human side altogether. They are brittle and stiff, and that limits their leadership influence and effectiveness.

When a leader opts out of the tension, her influence erodes. A Superstar speaks up about her opinion, which is real, but she is closed to the opinions of others. A Separator is both closed and hidden, meaning he doesn't speak up about his opinion and is not curious about the opinions of others. And while an Accommodator is curious and open to other people's points of view, she does not reveal what she thinks, feels, or wants in that moment. These are ineffective team conflict styles versus the effectiveness of the Influencer.

TEAM CONFLICT STYLES

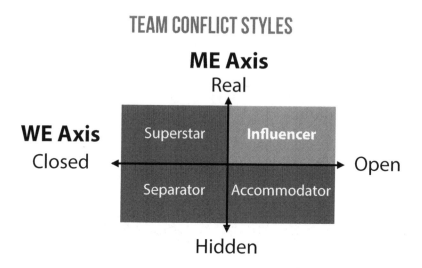

To be an influential and effective leader of people, you need to show up as a whole person. Don't treat yourself and others as machines. Use your natural resources: your heart, mind, and inherent willingness to engage. When you do, your people will follow suit. Your willingness to be vulnerable, curious, and courageous provides a powerful model for those you lead.

The challenge of leadership is to include your whole self. When you do, you have easier access to your own creativity and intuition. You connect more effectively with the people you lead because you are more congruent, increasing your influence with your people, and building trust and loyalty.

CHOOSING INFLUENCE

A few years back we coached Todd, the Executive Director of a large inner-city non-profit Community Center. His mission from the board was to introduce new youth programs to revitalize the center. He was met with resistance from long-time staffers. We discussed using both vulnerability and curiosity with this staff as keys to influence.

At an all-staff day, Todd invited the new youth program leaders to introduce their program to the rest of the staff by providing experiential activities to encourage buy-in from the rest of the staff.

As the youth program leaders kicked off the activities, a group of four older staff members sat back to observe. When Kelly, one of the youth program leaders, inquired about their decision, the response was, "We are too old for learning new tricks. Best we just watch." Kelly nodded and started to move on.

Todd immediately jumped up and challenged the group, "Hey guys come on! How can you resist this stuff?"

The group's spokesman, Frank, was about to disagree to the challenge when CrisMarie stepped in.

"Wait, Todd, can I check in with you?" Todd nodded.

"Just quickly, can you tell me how vulnerable you are being? Are you being real or hidden right now?" No one else had a clue what CrisMarie meant, but Todd did.

"Hmm, not much. I guess I'm showing up like an Accommodator. Let me try it again," Todd replied. CrisMarie nodded.

Todd took a breath. "Okay, what's real is that I am frustrated. I want you long-time staffers to give these youth programs a chance. You need to know the youth program is happening. This is the direction our mission is headed, and I'd like you to join us. If you choose not to, then I'm going to have to make tougher decisions."

The group was silent.

CrisMarie acknowledged Todd for being real and vulnerable and reminded him about curiosity.

"So, now you know where I am. I want to know why this is so challenging for you. I know I haven't been listening, and maybe now that I have gotten this off my chest, I can. Tell me what stops you from joining?"

The older staff were definitely surprised, and then Frank responded, "We thought you were going to fire us or replace our programs, and it sure seemed like all you were interested in was the new youth direction. Sounds like there is some truth to that."

Todd paused. "Yes, the youth programs are critical for getting grants and community support. But, I don't want to lose you guys. You have the most popular adult classes and activities. I just see you all as resisting everything I suggest, and I get frustrated."

The air and direction of the meeting had shifted, and productive dialogue ensued. The staffers tried some of the experiential activities and liked them! There was engagement and even input from the older staffers about how to make the youth programs successful with this community.

The shift occurred when Todd became vulnerable and curious. He became an influencer. It wasn't comfortable, but when he dared to use the tool, the entire meeting shifted. No one else needed the tool, but when Todd self-corrected, creative dialogue occurred.

BRINGING THE ME AND THE WE TOGETHER

We've focused on the ME in this section—the space within you. Often, people don't give this much thought. As a business leader, you may find yourself trying so hard to get tasks done and perform well that you don't pay attention to what drives you, what you're thinking (your assumptions about the situation), and how you really feel, other than *fine*. Without awareness of what is happening inside, you may repeat the same patterns, run into the same blind spots, and persist in the inability to break through the upper limit of your own success, effectiveness, or influence. Strength, vulnerability, curiosity, courage, congruence, pause, emotions—these are all tools to help you stay grounded in the ME.

When you discover what's true inside, you can bring it into the light of day. You can be more real with both yourself and others in the situation. When you choose to be real, you are congruent and authentic, and those around you respond to the difference.

If you want to learn more about the combination of vulnerability and curiosity and the power it creates on teams, check out our TEDx Talk *Conflict: Use It, Don't Defuse It!* on YouTube or at www.Thriveinc.com/beautyofconflict/bonus.

Let's move on to the WE—the space between you and another. The next section covers the tension that comes up inside yourself and between you and others when you each start sharing more fully what you truly think, feel, and want. To bring the ME and the WE together, you must know your own inner space and reveal your position with vulnerability while being curious and open to others. You can embody this type of leadership at home, at work, within communities, and anywhere in the world. When you do, you hold the key to expanding your influence in any circumstance.

In the section on the WE, we'll show you how to work through and be more effective when those tough conversations pop up on your team.

SECTION FIVE
The We

SECTION FIVE
OVERVIEW

The WE includes the ME and the other person, meaning relationships. We believe relationships matter as much as results and are in fact key to your results.

To engage the WE requires you develop the motivation, courage, and skills to engage with someone whose opinion is different from yours. This isn't always easy.

As a leader, it means creating a space or container within the team for the good, bad, ugly, and beautiful. Within this container, you can build and engage with the energy of conflict. This portion of the book gives you the frame of reference, tools, and tips for hanging in through difficult conversations so you can get to clarity and collective creativity on the other side.

WE focus develops your team's relational health and the ability to engage with each other directly, honestly, and in real-time. As a result, the trust, energy, inspiration, and engagement on the team skyrockets. The team better understands differences and clears up breakdowns that slow everyone down and stop forward momentum. When you focus on the WE, gossip, politics, and factions disappear. Your team is more connected, fulfilled, and engaged as trust and curiosity expand across relationships. Performance velocity accelerates.

Remember, creativity comes from the gaps between us, which are our differences. These gaps can lead to clashing, but that clash is where a leader must choose to opt in. Innovation results when these differences are explored, bent, twisted, and combined. Something new emerges that no one saw in the beginning. This is where the source of the team's competitive advantage emerges. This is the power of opting in.

The team's willingness to cycle through multiple oh, sh*t! moments expands as each person learns from every experience. Your team is better able to tolerate the tension and ambiguity of conflict. Together you produce innovative solutions to tough problems—not just once, but repeatedly.

As teams become more tolerant of tension and ambiguity, the differences on a team become valuable assets. Instead of avoiding the conflict and discomfort, team members dare to take more risk, and that generates collective genius. A team that just gets along or stays in a comfort zone may stay together, but it will miss the collective brilliance and competitive advantage that comes when differences are acknowledged, shared, twisted, tested, and used to reach new frontiers. Let's dive in and learn how.

CHAPTER 16
How To Have Tough Conversations Successfully

Some years ago a scientific company was in danger of losing government funding due to poor results. The CEO had tried to solve the issue with different project approaches. Then he realized the problem wasn't a bad project plan, or even bad people. The plan was solid, and these folks were smart. The problem was that his team wasn't working together. He called us.

We listened to his challenges then crafted an engagement that would take them through the first year and get them to successful completion of their government project. Throughout the year, we facilitated six off-sites. At the end of our first day of the first two-day off-site, CrisMarie and I chatted about one of the older team members.

"Drew hardly said a thing all day," CrisMarie said. "I could tell he was bored and disappointed in the day's events."

"He did seem a little disengaged," Susan replied.

"I don't want to push."

"Agreed. He was resistant to this whole team idea in the first place. Why don't we see how it goes tomorrow morning, and if he still seems disengaged, we'll check it out with him."

We both were certain Drew was an unhappy camper. And because we each came to that assessment independently, we felt confident we were right.

We didn't make any significant changes to the remainder of our session, and we were happy that Drew did speak up more as we continued. But what really surprised us was what happened when we asked for closing comments at the end of the two days. We both expected Drew to say something negative. To our surprise, when it was his turn, he sat up straight and his face lit up.

"This was the best two days I've ever spent at a team off-site in my career," he said with a smile. "We got more done than I ever expected, and I actually enjoyed myself."

So much for being right!

It is common for people to create a story about other individuals or situations with only limited information. Even coaches who help others avoid that trap aren't immune. We create a story, we believe that story, and we move forward without thinking otherwise.

We chatted with Drew as we were leaving at the end of the second day. We told him how we had interpreted his looking down and staying quiet as disengagement. We shared that we understood our interpretation was wrong, and how glad we were to learn something new about him. Drew's response?

"You know, my wife tells me that all the time," he said. "I never have been one to smile or make a big deal out of things. But she has taught me that I'd better say something, so I'm glad I spoke up. I imagine there are others like me, so I'm happy you learned something."

BE SURE TO CHECK

When you tell yourself a story about someone and assume you're right without giving the other person room to express, you almost always treat that person unfairly. It's impossible to know what is going on inside another person—how they think, feel, or what their motivations are—unless you explicitly check out your story. Only they can confirm what is happening for them on the inside.

Fortunately, in Drew's case, we didn't change the process or the outcome of the off-site. But we have to admit we were more cautious and guarded with Drew than we were with the rest of the team.

If we hadn't checked it out directly, we could easily have interpreted Drew's participation (or lack thereof) as wrong and created even more distance from him throughout the course of the engagement. Instead, we got new information and discovered Drew was on board.

The solution isn't to shut down the storytelling or judgments. It's sharing your judgments with vulnerability and curiosity—what we call 'Check It Out!'—that enables you to bridge the differences between people, build trust, and create greater engagement.

When you share your own interpretation or opinion, you reveal more about how *you* put the world together than about the other person or situation. That's why it takes vulnerability. You are revealing your own personal truth, and not *the* truth.

Most human beings have a desire to express who they are, to speak up honestly, and to show how they feel. People also want to be liked and accepted by the group. And there's the paradox and tension. We want to be understood, but also to control the situation and avoid rejection. Believing we're right is one way to stay in control. Letting go of the need to be right and revealing how we put the world together is like leaping without a net.

This is why people ask questions. When you ask questions, you remain safely hidden, not revealing your beliefs, just gathering new information. This seems like a great strategy, but when it is overused (as I, CrisMarie, have done over the years), you can end up thinking your opinion doesn't matter.

Come out of hiding. Find out if the story you've told yourself fits with others' experiences, and be open to their answers. That takes courage and curiosity.

By sharing your judgments, interpretations, opinions, assumptions, or theories as a *story*, and not claiming them as fact, you create a space for the other person to give you new information. This is the heart of closing the gap between team members and, in doing so, building trust. Share your story, then say, "Where do we agree or disagree?" Or, "Tell me where this doesn't make sense to you."

We use the term *story* to remind leaders that they make it up as they go along. We all do. Why not check to see what fits for the other person?

HOW TO BREAK IT DOWN

Have you ever been in a meeting and thought, "Great, we're all on the same page," only to find out everyone had a different interpretation of the same events? Or maybe, like we did in our interaction with Drew, you created a story about someone that was completely wrong?

Each person processes incoming information differently because everyone has different backgrounds and experiences that shape how they think. You aren't exempt. As humans, we attach meaning to what we hear, see, and experience. It's natural. The brain is a meaning-making machine. We make meaning through the data we take in and sort the data through our personal filter. Then we create a story, which drives how we feel. Just remember, everyone processes incoming information differently. Let's take a look at each of the steps of meaning making.

HOW HUMANS PROCESS[11]

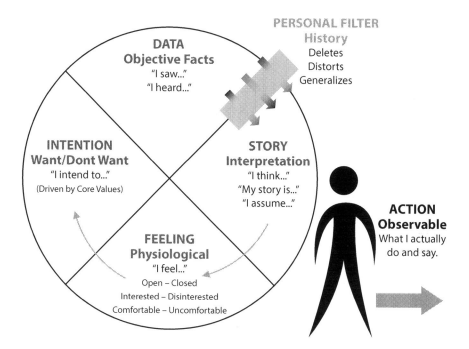

Data

You receive information or data through your senses: what you hear, see, taste, touch, and smell. In business, it is primarily limited to what you hear and see; although, we have worked for several food companies where tasting and smelling come into play.

Data is the objective information with no meaning attached. For example, I see someone who is crying and sad. This is not objective data. If I am truly objective, the more accurate statement is that I see someone who has tears on her cheeks, or even more objective, who has water on her cheeks. I don't know how she feels. Maybe she has allergies, or maybe there's dust under her contact lens.

Personal Filter

You take in data, and it is processed through your own personal filter. Your personal filter is made up of all that makes you unique: gender, age, where you grew up, past work history, and your significant emotional life events. Your brain sorts the data, labeling some things good and other things bad. You do this unconsciously. Say, for example, when you were young a small dog bit you. Ever since then you've been afraid of small dogs. Your brain and nervous system now categorize all small dogs as dangerous. Today, when you see a small dog, you immediately feel fear. For someone else, seeing a small dog might elicit a completely opposite or even neutral reaction.

As the information or data goes through your personal filter, your brain deletes, distorts, and generalizes information. That's why each member of a team can have different interpretations of the same event.

YOUR PERSONAL FILTER

Personal Filter

DATA Observerable Facts	History	STORY Interpretation
	Deletes	
	Distorts	"I think..."
"I saw..."		"My story is..."
"I heard..."	Generalizes	"I assume..."

Your Story

Data goes through your personal filter and out pops your story. Your story is your interpretation, hunch, opinion, assumption, theory, or judgment of the situation. Remember, we use the word *story* to emphasize that people make things up as they go. Your experience may strongly reinforce your story, but it's still your story just the same. Here are some examples:

"Joe's the smartest guy on our team." This is a story, not a fact. Your collected data may lead you to this conclusion (he speaks up quickly in meetings, always has data to back up his position), but still, it's only your opinion. To verify it as a fact, you could compare IQ scores. Even then someone else may bring a different type of smarts, such as emotional intelligence, to the situation.

"My boss does not like me, and he always gives me the hardest assignments." Maybe you can point to pieces of data that lead you to this conclusion, but still, it is just a story. You don't know how your boss feels about you unless you ask him. You may think you get the hardest assignments, but how do you measure that?

It's critical to notice that your story is your creation and that it's not necessarily true. And it's important to know that your stories drive your feelings.

Your Feelings

We generate feelings from the stories we tell ourselves. Feelings come in four major categories: happy, sad, mad, or scared. There are many variations on these four emotional themes, and we've made it simpler by reducing it to two categories. We focus on physiologically—relating emotions to the movement of energy in the body.

Our emotions are energy in our body. Similar to how the waves of the ocean ebb and flow, when we respond to something at a feeling level, we are either opening to it or closing it off; moving toward it or away from it. At the physiological level this can register as temperature change or a sense of distance between me and another. So we can feel warm toward someone or cold to them; close to them or distant from them.

One way of thinking about emotions is related to your physical location relative to someone else or someone's idea. Do you want to lean forward or lean back and cross your arms?

Let's experiment.

Start by bringing to mind someone you are fond of. What happens in your body? Do you open and soften? Do you feel warm? Do you notice yourself lean forward?

Now think of someone that you have a strong distaste for. What shifts in your body? Do you tighten or brace anywhere in your body? Do you get colder or notice a desire to back up or turn away?

This exercise helps you notice your own internal landscape. Everyone has their own unique physiological reaction. We encourage you to bring your awareness to how you feel in your body when you experience positive or negative events in your day.

FEELINGS ARE PSYCHOLOGICAL

Intention

From feeling we generate intention. Our intentions are what we want, desire, or wish for. We can have more than one intention in any given situation.

Example one: You're dealing with a difficult direct report. One intention might be to give feedback and ask for information about their poor project performance. Another intention might be to communicate that you are in charge, and he needs to do what you tell him without questioning you.

Example two: You're dealing with decision making on the team. One intention might be you intend to get input from your team, and another is you intend to make the final decision.

You may even notice your intentions shift in the moment. You may start with an intention to get input from your colleague, and as your colleague delivers information, you realize your intention is not to get input, but to simply relay your decision.

Check in regularly and notice your own shifting thoughts, feelings, and intentions.

As a meaning-making machine, recognize that you constantly sort data through your senses, and you attach your own meaning to the data. That generates how you feel. You cannot stop the data from coming in. Your brain is wired to receive it and translate it. We suggest that you be aware of the stories you tell yourself and consider that you may not be right. Make a point to check it out!

CHECK IT OUT!

Checking out your story with another person is the key to creating productive dialogue.

CHECK IT OUT

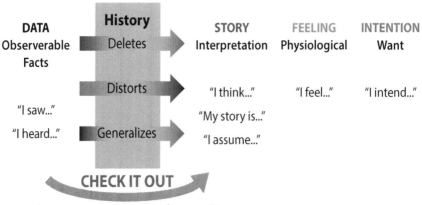

Personal Filter

DATA	History	STORY	FEELING	INTENTION
Observerable Facts	Deletes	Interpretation	Physiological	Want
	Distorts	"I think..."	"I feel..."	"I intend..."
"I saw..."		"My story is..."		
"I heard..."	Generalizes	"I assume..."		

CHECK IT OUT

"Do you agree? Do you disagree?"

To illustrate, we'll share a client story.

A national telecom client had asked us to design and implement a leadership-development program to help their team leaders become more effective by fostering creativity from conflict on their teams. During the three-day process, we had them practice *Check It Out!*

Two managers, Robin and Bernie, had worked together on a project at another company five years earlier. That project had failed, and both managers wound up leaving the company. Robin hated Bernie and blamed him for her own departure. Bernie didn't trust Robin.

When they collided with issues during our program, we challenged them to *Check It Out!* Here's how Robin checked out her story with Bernie:

> Data: "I heard you went to my boss and badmouthed me."
>
> Filter: "I worked my butt off for that project."
>
> Story: "My story is that you had it out for me and were the reason I was let go."

Feeling: "I'm angry."

Intention: "I want you to talk to me directly if you don't like something I have done, rather than go behind my back."

Check it out: "Do you agree that you did badmouth me to my boss?"

Bernie was shocked. He had been a supporter of Robin's years prior. That was until he heard she disliked him.

"Wow! I'm surprised. I thought *you* had undercut *me*," he replied. "I did talk to your boss about the challenges I had with our project. I didn't discuss you, though. I heard from others that you thought *I* was the problem. I never checked any of that out, and because of that, I thought of you differently."

Robin and Bernie came back from this five-minute exercise in a totally different space with each other. Five minutes of checking it out completely transformed their relationship.

When we assume our story about someone is true without checking it out with them, we may treat that person unfairly. We create distance and build walls. The relationship becomes brittle, and the team's productivity suffers.

We may take it even further by avoiding the person, gossiping about him, and swaying others to our point of view. This divisiveness is the root of politics, factions, and cliques that bond together to make someone outside of the group wrong. It snowballs as insiders continue to gather evidence that they are right. This creates more distance and dysfunction between the factions.

Break down the walls and distance by exercising the courage to check out your stories. Vulnerability and curiosity will enliven you. You will discover things you wouldn't learn otherwise because you can't know what is going on inside another person. It's impossible to know how someone thinks or feels, or what his motivations are, unless you explicitly check out your story and hear it from him.

Remember the earlier experiment with feelings? Whether your feelings are positive or negative, check it out and see what happens!

The next time you find yourself judging or being stuck in your opinion, don't shut down your imagination and creativity. Instead, remember to:

1. Speak up
2. Describe the data of how you came to your conclusions
3. Share your judgments *as a story*
4. Say how you feel
5. Include what you want
6. Check it out!

The possibilities are limitless. A narrow view of the world can restrict leaders from reaching their fullest potential. Having tough conversations opens our minds. When you reveal your perspective and check it out, you will most certainly discover new territory. Therein lives creativity, and that is the best path for continued learning and engagement.

If you want some more support on this topic, we have an easy step-by-step worksheet for you to follow called, *How to Have a Tough Conversation at Work*. Go to <u>www.Thriveinc.com/beautyofconflict/bonus</u> to download it now.

Next, we'll see how silence, even though it feels like the safe bet, is deadly—especially on a team.

CHAPTER 17
Silence is Deadly

Conflict is a hard sell. No one wants conflict, not even us. Unaddressed conflict fractures the WE of your team, especially if you as the leader have not provided your team with the skills and support to address it in a healthy way. When conflict shows up it creates discomfort and can break apart relationships and teams. Why, then, do we encourage conflict?

Because silence is even more detrimental than conflict.

Have you ever heard an idea at work and known it was either a bad suggestion or would cause more problems—and yet you said nothing?

You stayed silent because you didn't want to make a meeting last longer. Or you decided that maybe you were wrong, they were right, and everything would be fine. Perhaps the person you disagreed with was a longtime teammate, or even a friend outside of the office. Why upset the relationship?

Maybe nothing horrible happened, but what if it had?

When I, Susan, was in my twenties, I worked in a hospital as an anesthesiologist tech—essentially the social arm for the anesthesiologist and surgeon to the patient. I would meet with the patient outside the operating room and ask simple questions, check blood pressure, and make sure everything was set for the patient to go into surgery.

One patient was a woman about to have knee surgery. She told me how she had injured her right knee. The surgeon came in during our conversation, and I stepped back to let him examine her. He manipulated and poked at her left knee, and there was very little dialogue between them. Then he turned and went, and I came back to check in with the patient. "Didn't you tell me it was your right knee that needs surgery?" I asked.

"Yes," she replied.

"Did you mention that to him?" I continued.

"He knows," she replied, her voice a little wobbly.

"Hmm," I replied. I wasn't so sure.

I finished with the woman, and when I left her room, I noticed the surgeon standing nearby. I told him that I had been talking to the woman and wondered why he had been working on her left knee when it was her right knee that had been injured.

"Who the hell are you to tell me how to do my job?" he exploded. "You have no business even talking to me. Now, get out of my way so I can go operate."

I walked away, rattled.

I was done with that case, and the day proceeded as usual. I tried to recover my sense of grounding, but said very little to any other surgeons that afternoon. As I was leaving for the day, that surgeon stopped me.

"I shouldn't have jumped on you. I was out of line," he said.

I was so surprised that I grappled to find my words. "I'm sorry," I said. "I guess I just wanted to check. I should have realized you know your job."

"The truth is, if you hadn't said anything, I would've operated on the wrong knee," the surgeon replied. "I was in my operating mode and thought it was the left knee. She didn't say anything to correct me, so I didn't even give it another thought."

I was stunned. I appreciated his courage, vulnerability, and humanness to come back and apologize.

This is an extreme but powerful example. When people stay silent like that knee patient did, they risk negative impacts. It would be easy to blame the doctor's bullying style as the source of the problem, but the dynamic is much more complicated. The choice to stay silent can cause considerable damage.

Silence is one of the biggest problems in relationships, particularly on teams. Speaking up in tough situations is critical to smooth operations (no pun intended). Each of us helps perpetuate the bad behavior when we stay silent or blame another person in our heads or behind their backs. Silence makes us a victim and them the villain.

Silence on the outside doesn't mean silence on the inside. Our outer silence only masks the ongoing rant in our head. It keeps us from seeing our part in the problem, and that leaves the team's collective potential to the loudest person. In silence we abdicate our responsibility in the WE. We miss how *everyone's* role contributes to the outcome. It is easy to blame the bully, but on a team, silent members equally contribute to the dysfunction of the WE.

It's important to name silence as a part of the problem. Acknowledging it is critical to understanding that what appears obvious (that the problem is the bully or dominant team member) may not be the only issue. Too many teams focus solely on the bully, which is important, but it does not address the silence, which is crucial.

Silence, at its core, is failure to expose, express, or reveal a different point of view (i.e., conflict).

Lack of conflict in the health care industry can and does injure and kill people. In businesses, it stops creativity and innovation, creating a slow death for organizations. In business, conflict is usually less of a safety issue and more of a strategic issue.

Let's say you are facilitating a team meeting about a new product line. As the leader, you have a passionate opinion about the right direction. A brave soul speaks up to challenge your opinion—your *right* idea. You immediately react by challenging that person in return, and that creates a spark.

That spark is crucial! And it's uncomfortable, because we aren't used to confrontation or have not been taught how to tolerate it. But when we opt in to it, that spark ignites the flame of creativity and innovation. It generates new, creative ideas and solutions.

But let's say the brave soul decides in his head that you're right and he's wrong. "Never mind," he says. "I'm good with your plan."

Now his ideas, and the resulting new ones to emerge from the clash are lost. The team goes forward, operating on only your idea. You kind of like that, because it feels good to be right, and you revel in that feeling of rightness. The truth, however, is that new thinking has been pushed aside for you to get your own way. Hmm.

We have a strong desire to identify a right and a wrong. That right/wrong thinking is seductive. It makes us feel safe. It keeps us out of uncertainty, ambiguity, and the anxiety of the unknown. The world is clear, black and white.

But when you fall into the right/wrong trap, you don't foster new ideas. Hand-in-hand with the desire to *just get along,* the right/wrong trap deadens creativity, innovation, and possibility.

Frankly, there is no safe way to introduce conflict. There is, however, a compelling reason to do so, and it has a big upside.

Speaking up is worth the discomfort, even to the point of feeling anxious. If I'd not spoken up in the hospital, that poor woman would have had an operation on the wrong knee. I remember that situation every time I want to pull back into silence and safety. Even if avoiding conflict in your work or relationships won't cause physical pain or injury, the outcome of your silence will be a casualty.

So we sell conflict, even knowing it is a hard sell.

TIPS TO BREAK THE SILENCE

As a leader, it's your job to notice when people are uncomfortable and not speaking up. You may have to slow down the meeting or delay a critical decision to open the floor for naysayers and reluctant people to speak up.

Here are some things to say during a meeting where you pick up those signals:

- "I realize people may be hesitant to speak up because you think we're too far down this path to stop. I want to say right now, we can decide this is a no go. Nothing is off limits at this point."
- "I notice that Ted, Mary, and I have been doing most of the talking. It is so easy for us to carry on and for me to think everyone is on board. This is an important decision. So let's pause and check in with the rest of you individually."
- "I feel a sense of urgency about this project, and I may be shutting down dialogue with my desire to move ahead. I think we'd benefit from taking a step back and each identifying one potential risk to our current direction. Let's put our concerns on the table. I'll go first."

These are just a few examples of how a leader can step in and shift a longstanding pattern of silence.

It's important to do this regularly when a decision is coming to a critical point. And you may want to go first more than once to underscore for team members that it's okay to stop the momentum and speak up.

Did you know that in your greatest discomfort lies your greatest potential for creativity? Read on to learn more.

CHAPTER 18
Tense Moments Equal Creative Opportunities

Teams often rely on the loudest members' or leaders' ideas and experience. That might be good for business as usual, but it's neither innovative nor transformative.

The real solution to interrupting business as usual comes when people, especially the leader, are willing to risk having their own ideas challenged, rejected, or changed. Why would anyone do that?

People show up authentically and share their true thoughts because they understand that creativity and innovation is only possible when *my idea clashes with your idea*. In that clash is a real and honest opportunity for something totally new to emerge! Granted, showing up can feel uncomfortable and risky. That's why we start every coaching relationship by helping each team member understand himself and his own patterns. If you don't understand how you defend, interrupt, and cope to get away from tension, you will continue to interrupt or avoid the gap and the clash.

Once you understand your ME patterns, we encourage you to step forward into the WE and welcome the clash. Our hope is that you can know yourself well enough to see when you are caught in your defenses or you should step out of the way. When you understand that gaps and differences are the greatest opportunity for innovation, you will find the courage and heart to hang in and let your judgments be tested. You'll consider, listen to, and be influenced by one another, and therein lies great possibility.

Leadership demands a high level of self-mastery, because when you go first, you model vulnerability and curiosity. It takes courage to be real in your leadership role, but holding back or pretending everything is okay stops the flow of creative energy. Open the door to your creative energy and the team's with openers like this:

> "I think we aren't getting anywhere."
> "I'm not curious or wanting to be influenced right now."
> "I'm not comfortable, but I think this is important. Let's keep going."
> "I'm not sure any one of us is listening to the other."

Each of these disclosures demonstrates vulnerability and creates a path for others to follow. It clears the pathway for people to hang in and have faith. Yes, even when I say I'm not curious, I'm being vulnerable and something new can emerge.

When you check out your assumptions and rightness, you can get beyond what you think you know.

Earlier, we introduced our *Check It Out!* communication model. To get your own copy, download *How to Have Tough Conversations at Work* at www.Thriveinc.com/beautyofconflict.com.

The model helps facilitate conversations that focus on the gaps between us—our differences. However, as a tool it is only as useful as the intention of those who use it. That's why communication tools alone are not a solution. Even with helpful tools, our own blind spots get in the way of transformative interactions. Intentions for respectful and polite discussions don't lead to transformational conversation.

Transformation takes place when there is risk and uncertainty. This is the counterintuitive piece of the equation: are the leader and team willing to risk breaking apart? Is there a playing field in which people can bring all of themselves to the game, lose, and still keep playing while learning from mistakes?

Two internal conflicting drives make these types of transformative conversations difficult:

1. You want to be your own unique individual—the ME.
2. You want to fit in, stay connected, and collaborate—the WE.

These conflicting drives create incredible tension inside individuals and between people, yet this is just where creativity is discovered! In these tense moments, ask yourself, "Am I willing…

- to step into that space and remain curious about others and myself?
- to risk being influenced and changed?
- to be an individual (ME) in the face of others (WE)?
- let my reality shift?"

If the answer to any of those questions is no, you may not seriously be interested in the other. You're still invested in your reality, being right, and playing it safe. It is important for you to recognize this.

This is the paradox. It's the magic turning point. When you choose to own just how closed you are and share that out loud, your internal energy shifts.

Suppose that rather than pretend to be interested and listen to the other, you choose to be real and say, "You know, right now I am not that open and curious about you and your ideas." The energy inside you moves.

You are no longer ignoring your true position. You just said it. You don't have to pretend or fight it.

This is exactly what keeps the dialogue going. Yes, it is paradoxical. The very act of saying where you are means you are no longer still there. You're sharing your truth in the moment.

Sometimes the most powerful step is to say, "Right now, I'm not willing to be changed. Will you still let me stay in the game?" Imagine in business being that honest, raw, and real. You want that real honesty on your team. You need that real honesty on your team, and it takes tremendous courage and heart to hang in and be with each other in this way.

We worked with a team whose leader, Kip, was willing to take this courageous step and embrace the clash.

GET REAL

I, CrisMarie, did some executive coaching with Kip, the CEO of a technology company, for about four months. At that point he wanted support to resolve conflict between two of his six executive team members, Lucas, and Jay. Susan and I facilitated a two-day off-site. We were deep into day two, and the team had made significant progress when Donna, VP of Operations, challenged the CEO on the reoccurring issue.

"Look, I've heard you say that you want this conflict resolved between Jay and Lucas, but I think you just want Jay, and us, to be okay with Lucas," Donna said. "You like Lucas and, frankly, you let him do whatever he wants. That's the real issue."

Kip immediately jumped in. "Not the case. I will not make Lucas the target here. This is a team issue."

"Hey, I'm not making Lucas the problem here," Donna countered. "I'm saying *you* are the problem."

Silence.

CrisMarie spoke. "Look, Kip, you agreed to let us step in and give you feedback. I believe you really want to hear from your team. This may be hard, but I think their feedback is crucial to support the development of the WE—your team. Are you interested in hearing it?"

Kip huffed and said, "Yes, of course I'm interested."

What followed were details from team members about interactions that had occurred over the past six months. In each of the situations, Kip had given Lucas the go-ahead on a new project that crossed other's areas without getting the buy-in from the other team members.

Kip listened as the team members talked. It was clear from his facial tightness and locked jaw that he wanted to disagree. But he didn't.

Finally, he said, "I think what you're saying is that I give Lucas more room, and I don't include you in the planning of what he's doing when it's in your area? Is that the general message?"

Heads nodded. Kip paused, looking at the individuals sitting around the table, thinking.

He took a deep breath and spoke. "Look, Lucas is a fixer and always seems to make the business problem go away, but it makes sense that you would be upset if I have him poking around your areas. I wasn't thinking of the negative impact to the team." It was clear Kip and Lucas had created a mini-team and were solving business problems without the rest of the team. While this was good for the two of them, they were stepping on other people's toes, undermining team members' authority, and ultimately not helping the business.

The team was visibly relieved to hear Kip acknowledge what was happening.

Then Lucas spoke. "I have to admit, I know you let me do what I want. I haven't said anything because, quite frankly, I like it." The rest of the team was surprised by Lucas's admission. "But I know it has strained my relationships with you, Jay, and the rest of you, (he looked at the rest of the team). Which, I don't like."

Jay nodded and said, "Well stop sucking up to the boss then!" Laughter erupted in the room.

This was a powerful display of vulnerability and openness on the part of both Kip and Lucas.

Kip turned to Donna, who had brought up the issue in the first place. "I appreciate that you were willing to voice your opinion," he said, then turned to Lucas. "While I like the results you get, building a healthy team is critical, and I think we can do both." Lucas nodded once in understanding.

Kip then turned to the team. "I want you to call me out if you see me assigning Lucas projects that cross into your areas without involving you."

"Oh, don't you worry!" Donna chimed in, and laughter ensued.

This simple, real, honest conversation transformed this team, building their WE. It wouldn't have happened without the willingness of the team to speak up and bring forward their challenging and uncomfortable beliefs about their boss. Nor would it have made an impact if Kip had not been willing to own his ME, which in this case, was his ease in relating to Lucas and desire to do things differently.

The biggest team transformation occurs when the true issues are out on the table. It isn't easy, and it feels like a clash. These issues are not simply about business or strategy. They are personal or interpersonal. The personal factor is what makes being real feel risky, difficult, and potentially divisive. Still, it is those honest interactions that dramatically impact productivity and creativity.

Next, we'll give you a simple, concrete, and practical tool to turn around your team's performance in one hour.

CHAPTER 19
Turn Around Your Team's Performance in One Hour

Each individual on a team has a different idea about how team members should behave toward each other. Not only that, but unproductive habits emerge that undermine the success of the team. Unproductive behaviors are a precursor to poor business results. When you correct the behaviors, the team's business performance improves.

When we work with a client during a two-day team off-site, within the first day we can see these unproductive behaviors plain as day. Frankly, so can the team members. They just haven't openly discussed them as a group.

So we bring up the topic of team norms. Now, let's be clear: team norms are not rules that must be followed. Instead, they are behaviors that the team aims to adhere to, but without success, and this hinders productivity. We want the team to spotlight the negative impact of these behaviors so they are motivated and aligned to behave differently.

When we open the team-norm discussion, the most common bad behavior tossed out is lack of respect. This is a tricky one, because "respect" does not have a universal definition. As a team norm, there is already an issue about lack of clarity! Everyone defines respect differently.

Don't believe us? We'll use ourselves as an example because our clients aren't the only ones who confuse this word.

DIFFERENT DEFINITIONS OF RESPECT

We like positive or negative feedback in real time during team meetings. Yep, right in front of the team, because that shows respect for our clients. We don't want to waste your time, so we course correct in mid-stream if need be. And if we ask you to do it, we better also be willing to be vulnerable and real.

In our early working relationship, we weren't clear on our definition of respect. One afternoon, I, Susan, gave CrisMarie some feedback in front of a client's team.

"I notice you are repeating the same point," I told CrisMarie. "I think you're stalling, and we should move on."

Well, if looks could kill, I wouldn't be here to tell you about it. She was so flipping mad at me. When we debriefed on a break, I got an earful about how disrespectfully I had treated her.

"You made me look like a fool in front of the entire team!" she said. Hmm, that's not what I thought, but it was clearly what she thought.

Later, on the flight home, CrisMarie pulled out her notes. I thought she was going to type up the off-site team notes. But no, instead, she turned to me and said, "I have some feedback for you from the off-site. Are you open to hearing it?"

Of course I said yes. When she was on her third item, I started to squirm. When she hit her fifth point and was still not done, I got pissed.

"Really? You are telling me this now?" I said. "I have no time to recover.

Plus, if you thought this then, other people in the room were probably thinking the same thing! You let me hang out to dry without having the respect to tell me in real time so I could do something about it? I didn't even get to hear how it was for others in the room!"

We both had a visceral sense of our different definitions of respect. Clearly, the definition is not universal. We each have our own sense of it. And if my definition of respect is right, it makes hers wrong. Somehow, that's disrespectful in itself.

When we help teams define their team norms, we ask them to clarify the choice of *respect* by defining the word. The two most common responses are:

- To be polite
- To be nice

It may feel counterintuitive, but being polite and nice is far from being respectful. In fact, that behavior is a team effectiveness killer! Why?

When teammates are polite, they're usually holding back. That doesn't help the team, and it will quickly undermine the team's performance and the leader's effectiveness. When people make a conscious effort to be nice, they typically leave out what they really think. Instead they water down their point of view. The team misses out on valuable input and is less able to benefit from everyone's smarts.

Sometimes the truth does sting. But wouldn't you prefer honest feedback from a teammate than after the fact from a client, customer, a performance reviewer, or worse, an executive coach brought in from outside to tell you that your leadership style is problematic? (Yes, too often we have been paid to deliver the message a nice and polite team or boss would not!)

Don't get us wrong, we are not suggesting rude and mean become the alternative. Our suggestion is that teams feel free to aim for real and messy, with a commitment to clean up the mess. Don't let your team fall prey to nice and polite. Step in, say what's true, and clean it up if you mess it up! That is the fastest way to build team trust and have healthy conflict.

Say what's true and be curious about the impact—how's that for a great definition of respect?

Today, when CrisMarie and I lead team off-sites or leadership events, we employ a hybrid definition around feedback that we both feel comfortable using. We give real-time feedback to each other while we work with you, the client. And when it feels too uncomfortable or will take too long to discuss, we have the conversation on a break or at the end of the day. For me, this is vastly better than waiting for the plane ride home!

What are your team's norms?

DEVELOPING AND LIVING YOUR TEAM NORMS

To increase your team's performance, identify what behaviors help the team and what behaviors hinder the team. People on your team may have very different points of view on what works for the team and what doesn't. This makes for rich discussion. When CrisMarie and I talked about this, we learned a lot about each other's styles and preferences, and how we could work together more effectively.

Here are five steps to develop powerful team norms, increase team performance velocity, and live happily with your team:

1. **Brainstorm: What's working? What's not?** Brainstorming helps identify unproductive team behaviors. Because you want everyone—both introverts and extroverts—to participate, give people a few minutes to collect their thoughts and write on their own paper what they think is working on the team and what isn't.

2. **Discuss the impact.** Have a conversation about the items on the What's Not Working list. Prompt the discussion with

questions like, "How does this impact the team?" Or, "Why is this a problem?"

This impact discussion is an important step, because people are unconscious of how their unproductive behavior affects their peers. This discussion inevitably reveals root causes of problem behaviors, and that helps determine creative solutions.

3. **Pick the top three**. There may be five or ten important items to work on with your team. However, it's cumbersome to try to improve more than three areas. When you focus on everything, nothing improves.

4. **Turn it around.** In this step you will identify the desired positive behavior. Take a simple one like *people are late to meetings*. The opposite and team norm might be: *Show up on time*. Because you have had the impact discussion, this norm carries more substance.

Avoid vague concepts such as *be respectful*. As we saw earlier, people have different definitions for respect. If vague concepts come up, be sure to include specific definitions in the discussion. For example, for one team *be respectful* might mean *don't interrupt*; for another it might mean *be direct and don't speak behind other people's backs*.

5. **Hold the team accountable.** Here's where the rubber meets the road. Without this step, the impact of the previous four steps dwindles away. It is the leader's job to model accountability. The leader must be aware of, and actively and publicly address, when someone behaves counter to the top three norms.

Holding someone accountable doesn't mean punishing someone. Instead, it means stating the data and using the *Check It Out!* tool with curiosity. For example, "Tom, I notice you're walking in ten minutes late to our meeting, and we have a team norm to show up on time. I'm curious what happened?"

Tom probably has a good reason for being late. If not, he will likely change his behavior. In any case, the rest of the team will appreciate that you, the leader, hold everyone to the same high standards.

Once you, the leader, have modeled holding people accountable you want to cultivate what we all hated in high school: peer pressure or peer accountability. You want to set the expectation that team members hold each other accountable for the team norms as well. This is a natural development for the team when we work with them over time.

We'll go into team norms in more detail in Chapter 27, "Make Your Meetings Matter," where we talk about norms in relation to meetings. Watch your team performance increase as you have the courage to hold your team to higher standards—three norms at a time!

Do you really listen when people talk? Let's see how the power of listening can increase your team's IQ.

CHAPTER 20
Increase Your Team's IQ

Do you listen well? People often fight so hard to be heard that they don't pause and listen, I mean *really listen*, to what someone else has to say. It is easy to focus on stating our opinion rather than get clear about the opinions of others. Yet effective listening is the key for teams in building the WE and generating creative and innovative ideas.

To listen effectively requires an openness to be influenced. When you pause and really listen, you let in the other person's idea. Their perspective works on you, influences your feelings, and evolves your thinking. This sparks generative ideas, creativity, and innovation. Steven Covey put it well when he said, "Seek first to understand, then to be understood." We say, listen to understand, then respond.

PROMOTING VERSUS INQUIRING

People focus so strongly on promoting and advocating for their idea that they talk, rather than listen and inquire to clearly understand the other person's idea. On teams this often looks like the leader or the loudest member dominating the conversation. When this happens it limits the team's IQ, which is their resources to make decisions.

If you think of each person as having their own IQ (e.g., meaning smarts, emotional intelligence, organizational experience), you want to access their IQs when solving problems and making decisions. If you think of the team's IQ as a pool of those individual IQs, you want to make sure that pool is as large as possible when solving problems and making decisions.

When you have the loud extroverts or the leader dominating the discussion and not listening, it limits the size of that team IQ. It's as if the water gets splashed out of the pool as they dominate, and the other members go silent and opt out.

SHRINKING TEAM IQ

We commonly see this behavior the first time we join a team discussing a key topic. Let's look at one team meeting facilitated by a fictional character, Ethan.

Ethan leads a leadership team of a mid-sized manufacturing company. Five people sit around the conference table, yet it is only Ethan (the president), Alison (head of sales), and Dean (in charge of manufacturing) who speak. The purpose of the meeting is to determine how to meet the needs of their new product success. Listen to the tail end of their weekly tactical meeting:

Alison makes a passionate plea: "Our demand is high! My buyers want more of our product now, or else they'll go to our competitor. We need more product faster."

Ethan, the CEO, paces the room, staring at the ground. "I hear you, but that isn't our biggest issue," he replies, almost to himself. "We should be looking at our pricing and making adjustments."

"More product and higher prices?" Dean pipes up. "Really, people? No way. I am having a hard enough time keeping up production demand. If we don't slow things down and do some maintenance on our production line machines, quality is going to suffer."

The other two people in the meeting remain quiet. One pulls out his iPhone and checks his email.

Alison speaks up again, staunchly fixed in her opinion. "I still say the main issue is that we need more product now."

Ethan decides to call it. "Okay. I hear you. We need to make a decision and time's running out, but we have to end this meeting now. Let's table this. Just know we need to make a decision by next week."

Does it sound to you like they're hearing each other? Are they even focused on solving the same problem? They certainly have different ideas of what needs to be done, but who would know? There is no active inquiry. The ones who even speak are only stating their case, and the others remain mute.

The biggest listening cop-out in the history of business is, "I hear you." Does this sound familiar?

When we suggest people pause to listen to each other, they say, "I hear you." This is not listening. Instead, it's usually code for, "Yeah, yeah, I've got it. Now let me tell you my idea."

In the above example, this team could wait a week, but they won't get any closer to a good decision unless they choose to listen to each other. Listening is the major missing ingredient in the meeting.

A NEW INTENTION FOR LISTENING

We know it is a challenge to listen, especially when the person talking says something you disagree with or circles back to the same points. At this point, you probably stop listening, and your mind spins to come up with a strong counter argument to reinforce your position. It feels like war.

Instead of building your next line of defense, imagine listening with your mind and heart open to being changed. We know, this feels threatening, right? You could lose. But what if it isn't about winning or losing? What if it's about getting to the best, most creative, innovative idea? Ah, a different purpose—a purpose that supersedes you or me.

Wow! If this were the starting point for listening, how conversations would go differently!

Now, we don't mean you should abandon your own opinion, no! You already heard us say: "Be judgmental!" Smart people are. Go ahead and have your opinion. Just know that the conversation can't be creative if you're fixed on only your opinion, fighting to be right, and unwilling to be influenced by others. As a matter of fact, it's not much of an opinion if it's not strong enough to be tested, suspended, bent or twisted by teammates who are as smart and passionate about the vision as you are.

So, yes, have your opinion. But, also be willing to fully consider and try on someone else's opinion.

Actor and screenwriter Alan Alda's observation perfectly connects to our position on curiosity. He says, "Real listening is a willingness to let the other person change you. When I'm willing to let them change me, something happens between us that's more interesting than a pair of dueling monologues." Don't you love that?

Studies show that when an individual is able to share his story and be heard—meaning, when the listener can not only reflect back the speaker's words, but can demonstrate curiosity or empathy for the message content—the speaker is more likely to shift his position.[12,13] This is the true source of transformation and influence.

Likewise, we find that when leaders and teams listen to each other, they dramatically increase their team's IQ—the resources or information on the table that's then available to support better decisions. As a result, they are much more likely to come up with creative, innovative solutions. And those solutions are better implemented because they have the buy-in from team members around the table.

EXPANDING TEAM IQ

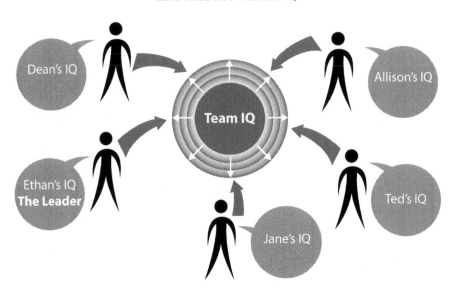

Teams who practice the art of effective listening generate innovative ideas not just once, but repeatedly. That's because team members show up with their own unique opinions, which are a necessary raw ingredient for creativity and innovation. When each person listens fully—with the intention of being influenced—people feel heard. When people feel heard, they loosen their tight grip on their opinions and allow ideas to merge, twist, and transform into something new.

Let us be clear: we are not talking about getting to consensus. We are talking about taking the time to hear and consider the different viewpoints around the table. Adults don't always need to get their way, but they do need to feel heard and genuinely considered. When people are heard and considered, they more easily support the decision of the team, even if it is not their initial idea.

BECOME A POWERFUL LISTENER

Do you want to become a powerful listener? We hope so, because it will go a long way toward increasing your influence as well as your team's IQ. Listening enhances your team's ability to make better decisions, innovate, and implement new ideas together.

Here are three critical steps to improve your listening:

1. Check your intention
2. Catch the ball
3. Demonstrate empathy

1. Check Your Intention: Are You Willing to Be Influenced?

When you listen with the willingness to be influenced, you show up differently. Willingness is evidenced through the statements people make and the questions they ask. For instance, when you are curious and interested in another person's idea and want to understand it clearly, you are more likely to slow them down with questions such as:

> "Wait a minute. I'm not sure I understand what you're proposing. Can you explain it again?"

> "Can you tell me how you came to that conclusion?"

Improve your willingness to be influenced by asking:

- Am I defending my position right now?
- Am I worried about being right?
- What's our mutual goal in this discussion?
- Am I willing to try on their point of view?

These questions support you to create a path to the place where you are willing to be influenced.

2. Catch the Ball, Pause, and Toss It Back

Catching the ball and tossing it back means taking the time to reflect back what you hear the other person say. This does not mean simply repeating the words or data, though that is part of it. It means paying attention to the possible emotions and intent underlying what's actually being said. Catch the words, as well as the heart and soul of your teammates' views, by taking two steps.

First, catch the ball (the person's idea) and hold it for a moment. This helps ensure you really understand the other person's idea or point of view before firing something back. The pause is important! We've sat in so many meetings where people think they are talking about the same thing, but from the outside it's clear they're misinterpreting each other and arguing completely different points. Pausing helps you digest the other person's opinion.

Second, toss the ball back by reflecting what the person is saying so that he feels heard. When someone feels heard, they more easily relax in their position and are open to hear your opinion. This creates buy-in on a team.

Tossing the ball back could sound like:

"So, do you mean [reflecting back your understanding of their position]?"

"I get that you're upset. It sounds like you're annoyed because you don't think I care about the project. Does that fit?"

"I want to make sure I'm following you. You think we're trying to solve a problem before we understand it. Is that right?"

When you do this, you validate what the person said. You show that what they think and feel is important enough for you to slow down and anchor it. They feel heard and important.

3. Demonstrate Empathy: 'No Wonder'

You've checked your intention, you've caught the ball and tossed it back. Now, finish strong. Take a walk in the other person's shoes. Even if you don't agree with her position, are you willing to understand how she put the pieces together? Can you appreciate if that's her story even if she's feeling how she is? It's not agreeing, simply seeing it from her perspective.

In our Individual IQ example, Ethan might have said to Alison, "Wow, sounds like you are getting pressure from your buyers to give you more or else they'll walk. No wonder you are so stressed. I don't want you to lose the business either."

That may feel like overkill—and maybe in a team meeting, it is. But, sometimes taking that extra step builds trust. And that shows up later as buy-in—even when someone doesn't get his way in the end.

If nothing else, be curious. Ethan could have said to Dean, "I had no idea we were taking our production to the limit. I know with your quality background that has to be difficult. What do you need in terms of maintenance time to feel solid about quality?"

When people believe you understand how they feel and why it is so important to them, they no longer have to fight to be heard. The energy of the conversation shifts. Often that frees up the discussion to move forward into problem solving.

What if you're the one who needs empathy? If you're frustrated and believe other people are not listening to you, or people keep doing something different than you're directing them to, you can always ask, "What are you hearing me say?" This gives the other person a chance to reflect their understanding of what you've said.

We are all busy, passionate, opinionated people. But remember, each of us wants others to consider our ideas worthwhile. Improve your listening by checking your intention, catching the ball and tossing it back. And, by all means, demonstrate empathy. We promise it will make a difference for the people you lead and work with.

Now, what do you do when you are dealing with someone who's defensive? Read on to find out.

CHAPTER 21
Deal with Defensiveness in Three Easy Steps

When someone criticizes something you care deeply about, it is natural to want to defend your belief. Instead, how can you move through that defensiveness and get to productive dialogue?

We had a long-term engagement with the executive team of a mid-sized consumer products company. At the previous two-day off-site, the team decided they wanted to look at expanding into new markets. Hunter, who was head of product development and a newer member of the team, volunteered to investigate options. Everyone appreciated that. He said he would present back at the next monthly half-day strategic meeting.

We facilitated the monthly strategic meeting's afternoon agenda, which addressed the topic of new markets. Hunter set up his computer and slides, then stood up and kicked off his presentation. He was enthusiastic about the possibilities as he went through a detailed PowerPoint presentation of his team's findings. He finished his presentation and looked out at his team.

Ten faces stared back at him. None of them appeared to be on board with his analysis. In fact, most seemed skeptical. Rather than the accolades or positive feedback Hunter had expected, he was met with, "Are you sure your data is correct?" This came from Bob, the CFO.

Tracy, the head of sales, piped up with energy, "Even if the data is correct, I don't agree with your interpretation of it."

Hunter immediately raised his defenses. "You guys don't understand. I've spent hours on this project!" He crossed his arms and his posture was stiff.

"Geez, Hunter, don't get defensive! We're just giving you our feedback," Bob retorted.

Can you guess what Hunter's response was?

"I'm not getting defensive!" Hunter said a bit too loudly and abruptly.

This is where we stepped in, but before we tell you about it, let's talk about defensiveness.

Hunter is not alone. There is a myth that some of us are defensive and some of us are not. Wrong!

We all get defensive. Don't believe me? Imagine something you have a large investment in, care deeply about, or have pride in. It could be a business idea, an article you've written, something you have created by hand, your home, your spouse, or even your child. Now, imagine someone you thought would provide positive feedback is instead critical, disagrees, or isn't supportive. Ouch!

When you feel that someone or something you care deeply about is being criticized, it's only natural (and even healthy) to feel defensive. Admittedly, this doesn't go a long way to foster healthy dialogue.

Neither does it feel good to be on the other side of someone else's defensiveness. What started as a conversation suddenly feels like a battle that you didn't expect. The friendly free-flow of ideas stops, and it feels like you've run into a brick wall, or that someone has shoved you right in the chest. Your immediate instinct is to defend and push back. This is where the phrase, "Don't get so defensive!" is used as a weapon.

Back to our original question: How do you move through defensiveness to get to productive dialogue? Whether you are feeling defensive or witnessing it, here are simple steps to help you move through it.

THREE STEPS TO DEAL WITH DEFENSIVENESS

Whether you get defensive (like Hunter), or you see someone else being defensive (like Bob and Tracy see Hunter), there are some surefire ways to move through it to healthy dialogue. Here are two scenarios nearly anyone can relate to.

Scenario one: You interpret someone's behavior as defensive.

Rather than say, "Stop being so defensive!" which only increases the person's defensiveness, try these three steps:

1. Reflect the gist of what you think the other person is experiencing, saying, and how you think they might be feeling.
2. Pause and let them respond. This allows them to vent the pressure they feel inside.
3. Empathize. Envision yourself in that person's shoes, and express your appreciation for how they feel.

We suggested Bob try this out with Hunter.

Bob opened with, "Hunter, it sounds like you're frustrated that I'm questioning your data and Tracy is questioning your interpretation of the data. Does that fit for you?"

Hunter responded, "Heck yeah! I worked my butt off on this and think both my data and interpretations are spot on. I'm pissed that you only seem to be interested in criticizing my work!"

Knowing that Hunter is new, that he wants to succeed, and that he put a lot of work into the project, Bob followed up with, "Hey, if I had put so much time and effort into my initial project with the team, and the first thing I heard was people questioning me, I'd feel frustrated too." (Good job Bob!)

This acknowledges that Hunter has good reason to feel the way he feels. Acknowledgement validates Hunter's feelings. He can shift from defending to listening. Now he'll either ask for what he needs or be more open to what the other folks in the room have to say.

Scenario two: You feel defensive.

When the shoe is on the other foot, and you are the one feeling defensive, here are three steps you can try if your teammates are not as adept at dealing with defensiveness. Hopefully, you do this before you react. Here are your three steps:

1. Reflect what you are hearing people say.
2. Acknowledge the impact on you; meaning, what is happening inside of you. If you skip this step, you may be subject to more of their criticism before you are ready to hear them.
3. Ask for what you need in order to be open to what you interpret as criticism.

Let's see how Hunter could use this technique with the team if he had a do-over.

Hunter, who's feeling tense inside, does not blurt out an angry response. Instead, he says, "Wow! So let me see if I have this correct. Bob, you disagree with the data, and Tracy, it sounds like you disagree with my conclusions. Hmm. I have to say, this isn't easy for me to hear. Actually, I feel quite defensive and want to push back, but I'm going to try not to. What would help me is to first hear if there is anything anyone does agree with."

This buys Hunter time to recalibrate internally and try to be open to the feedback. He can take a breath here to settle the ME in the face of a disagreeing WE. And it lets his teammates know that while they have their own opinions, the way they deliver feedback isn't working for Hunter.

The team update: When the team got through the defensive hiccup, Bob had some good questions about the data for Hunter. Indeed, some of it was outdated, which Hunter could not have known without getting new information from Bob.

Also, when Tracy shared her different interpretation about the data, it opened up a whole new conversation where more possibilities emerged. Over the course of the next three months, the team worked together to look at new market options. In the end they chose to expand into two new markets over the course of the next two years. At last account, those markets were doing very well!

Remember, the WE involves hanging in with yourself and the other person, and that gets messy. Most people don't like feeling defensive or being around someone who is caught in defensiveness. However, defensiveness is a natural response when you think something you care about is being attacked. Don't expect it to go away. Instead, learn how to navigate through it.

If someone else is being defensive: reflect, pause, and empathize.

If you feel defensive: reflect, acknowledge, and ask.

Deal with defensiveness like this, and you move through it to clarity and collective creativity on the other side.

Want to know the secret of improving your team performance? Read on.

CHAPTER 22
The Power of Team Accountability

Olympic basketball final match, 2008, Beijing, China: USA versus Spain. Score: 85-86. Time left on the clock: 35 seconds.

Chris Paul has the ball and is coming up court. He dribbles to the top of the key and sees Kobe Bryant open on his right. Just as he's ready to pass, Kobe's iPhone goes off.

Kobe grabs the phone, looks at who's calling, and answers. He holds up a finger so that Chris will hold the pass.

Time runs out. Gold medal: Spain.

You laugh. No way would Kobe have a phone on the court, and even if he did, he'd never take that call. But let's imagine that the US team played basketball the way business leaders today run their businesses. Get the point? If executives played in the Olympic games, not only could this happen, but based on the way business leaders live by their smartphones, it would probably be the norm.

Why? Because most business leaders aren't called out for their unproductive behaviors. Interrupting a meeting to look at an e-mail or pick up a call is disruptive 100 percent of the time. What's more, it's unnecessary and disrespectful to the person who is right there, face-to-face, giving you his precious time.

On the other hand, teams that hold each other accountable for unproductive behaviors outperform those that don't. Unproductive behaviors are the precursor to unproductive results. When leaders model, and teammates are willing to give direct, honest feedback on what is not working, then behaviors change, results improve, and the entire team is raised to a new performance standard.

BREAK THUMPER'S FATHER'S RULE

We encourage you to break Thumper's father's rule, from the movie *Bambi: If you can't say somethin' nice, don't say anything at all.*

That rule destroys teams and relationships! Relationships don't break down because of the major differences between people. It might look that way, but by the time major differences show up, there have been tons of little annoyances that were never addressed. Those little things that went unspoken will lead to the big chasm. On teams it's more important, even necessary, to encourage corrective feedback.

Back to Thumper and the real message to take away: If you don't have anything nice to say, it is probably because you have needed to say something not so nice for a long time.

Most people want the truth. They want honesty, even when it stings. They especially want it from their teammates. As you might remember, CrisMarie and I (Susan) had to learn how to share the hard stuff. It didn't work at first when I shared my feedback in front of a client, and she shared hers first on the plane ride home. We had to learn how to speak up to each other based on our different styles. Neither of us was happy to hear how we'd underperformed, but we got past that discomfort and were able to have a real conversation about how to communicate in the future.

Here's the thing. When you don't deal with the little things and clear them up, you wind up collecting other little bits of information that make that unproductive issue bigger and bigger.

Let's say your business partner, Archie, isn't great at getting all the details down after taking a call. You don't say anything, because you don't want to make a big deal of it.

It happens again. Still, it's no big deal. You shake it off. You did get the message, and even though there was no number attached, you have an address book so you can make it work. At least that's what you tell yourself.

Then you notice other little details Archie missed such as his expenses from his last trip, and the next steps he's responsible for in closing a client. And recently, you heard from a client that she was annoyed that you didn't get back to her in a timely manner. Surprised and embarrassed, you realize that it was a call Archie forgot to mention altogether!

You see how it grows. Now you have quite a case for Archie's poor behavior.

Just imagine how that conversation will go. You will work to control your edge as you blurt out a laundry list of details that Archie has delinquently forgotten, and you blame Archie for your client being upset with you because of Archie's poor behavior!

Trust us, it won't go well, nor will it be helpful. There is a better way.

Imagine saying something when the first instance occurs or shortly afterward. We know; that's radical.

"Archie, I'm uncomfortable bringing this up," you might say, "but I noticed my phone messages don't have all the details. I think you may be leaving out important information. This doesn't work well for me. I wonder if you've noticed that this has happened now a couple times?"

Archie may get defensive (see the previous chapter for some advice if this happens). Archie may disagree. However, you're being honest and clear with him, and this early in the process you may still be able to hear Archie's perspective and even come up with a better system that works for both of you.

It helps to remember, if it were you: Would you want to hear straight feedback early, or would you want people to hold back, talk behind your back, and wait until the problem is bigger?

HOLD YOUR TEAMMATES ACCOUNTABLE FOR BEHAVIORS

Great results come when team members hold each other accountable. If team accountability doesn't exist, the members will dissolve into mediocre performance.

When we say *accountability,* we don't mean just holding someone accountable for deliverables. Most leaders are comfortable with doing that. 'Archie, you were supposed to get that report to me on Monday. It's Wednesday. Where is it?'

Instead, we mean holding your team members accountable for unproductive behaviors. As we've explored, unproductive behaviors are precursors to unproductive results and unproductive teams! Teams that master giving and receiving regular, direct, honest feedback are rare— and, frankly, the highest-performing.

Don't let down your team by not speaking up early, even when it's hard. Wouldn't you want to know if what you were doing were causing problems? And wouldn't you want to hear it first from someone who cares?

Let's pick on someone besides Archie. Imagine that you are on the fictional IT team of Isaac, Martha, and Boyd.

How do you hold your teammates accountable? We help teams build a culture that holds members accountable in real time during team meetings. We have the leader model this behavior, which helps the team build the capacity to hold each other to these standards. In this way, people know that their behavior matters. It holds everyone to the same standards and saves a lot of time. However, most teams are not comfortable starting there. So with your fictional IT team, we suggest you start by making your move the same day Issac wasn't on his best team behavior during your team meeting when Martha gave a presentation.

Start with:

1. Context: Where and when it happened.

"Isaac, in our staff meeting this morning...."

2. Data: What you saw or heard him do.

"I noticed you checking your e-mail on your iPhone during Martha's presentation. You also jumped up to take a call when the team was trying to come to a resolution about Boyd's department."

3. Impact: Your story and/or feelings about the behavior.

"I thought your e-mail checking interrupted the flow of Martha's presentation. As for the call, when you left the room, the team stalled in making the decision because we needed your input. Now we have to come back to that discussion next week. I'm frustrated because I think it slows our team down and wastes a lot of time."

4. Curiosity: Check out what is going on for him.

"I'm curious, are you aware of your impact? Do you agree or disagree?"

Isaac may get defensive, or he may be surprised because he didn't realize the impact his actions had on the team and on you. If you just want to make Isaac wrong, the conversation won't go well. But if you sincerely speak up to address a behavior you think doesn't serve Isaac and the team, you are right on track.

People tell us, "I don't want to be the first one to speak up. I'm afraid I'll get fired." We won't lie, people do sometimes suffer consequences for speaking up, especially to difficult bosses. Even good bosses are taken by surprise, embarrassed, and react when someone critiques their behavior. It is human nature to want to be seen as competent. Being held accountable is not comfortable. There's a reason we address this topic here and not at the beginning of the book. It takes time to help the leader and the team build this capacity.

If you are a team member and not the leader, we suggest you first propose the question about holding each other accountable at a team meeting. Then you can hear what others think, including your leader. You can air your concerns, discuss what support the team needs to build this ability, and even ask the leader, "How do we talk to you when we are uncomfortable with your behavior?"

Whether in sports or business, giving feedback and holding your peers accountable for unproductive behaviors is the key to improving team performance. And yes, as a leader, you need to model this behavior so that the team picks up the ball. When you do so, people know it's safe and expected to provide feedback and to hold each other accountable for unproductive behaviors.

Now that you are equipped with new ME and WE abilities, let's move to the piece you have been waiting for—solving tough business problems.

SECTION SIX
The Business

SECTION SIX
OVERVIEW

In this section, we will help define the playing field—the business—in which you (the ME) and your team (the WE) operate. To do that, we provide key strategic and tactical questions that define the why, what, how, and who of your specific business. Asking the right questions will help your team gain clarity and collective creativity as well as find alignment with each other. When you and your team answer these crucial questions from your minds and hearts, the results are rarely rational and objective. Instead, you access creativity, inspiration, and innovation. Any conflict that arises in this process is the power source for creativity on your team.

COLLECTIVE CREATIVITY PATH

You want this conflict. You need this conflict.

Properly handled, conflict increases your team's IQ and capacity for powerful solutions for your business. The answers to the questions we'll share in this section become a resonant chord by which the team and the rest of the organization will live. The business becomes a living, breathing, multi-dimensional organism all pulsing together.

You may be wondering *why hasn't the business been the main focus of the book?* After all, it's what most business leaders talk about first. And, often, *all* they're interested in investing is their time and money.

We believe teams and businesses need to be healthy and smart. In fact, if you focus on the business, the smart side, without also understanding and developing the healthy side, yourself, then your team, and your team's engagement remains one-dimensional, like a machine without a heart. That's because the heart of a business is its people. People are the billows that inspire and fuel the heartbeats of the business. By nature, people are complicated and far from one-dimensional. As untidy as that can be, a business will fail or remain flat without the resiliency of people to flex and grow as time and space demands.

Start by attending to yourself (the ME) and develop vulnerability and curiosity. You and your team will engage in more healthy, open, and honest conversations (the WE). From there, talking about the business, the smart side, is inspired with e-motion (energy-in-motion).

That's why we have waited until now to talk about the business. It's important to make sure your organization first has the energy to fully come to life. Next up, learn why some businesses are so successful.

CHAPTER 23
Why Are Some Companies So Successful?

Why drives the business. A company is in business to make money, but something deeper is more compelling and inspiring than *just* making money—the big *why*. Several great thinkers before us have written about the big *why*: Simon Sinek put it most succinctly with the title of his book, *Start with Why*.[14]

In *Built to Last*, authors Jim Collins and Jerry Porras, framed it as this: "[It's] the organization's fundamental reason for being.... An effective purpose reflects the importance people attach to the company's work—it taps their idealistic motivations—...and gets at the deeper reasons for an organization's existence beyond just making money."[15]

The big *why* is that lofty impact you may realistically never achieve, yet it inspires, guides, and motivates the entire organization to a higher purpose.

For example, our *why* is *to change the way corporate America communicates*. However, we may never change the way all of corporate America communicates. When we work with an executive or leadership team, they come away with a whole new sense of how to improve their business through better communication with each other and within the entire organization. We know we are having an impact!

Companies built around a compelling and emotional *why,* are companies in which people are committed to working together even through the rough spots. The purpose of these organizations is strong enough that they will opt in to conflict in order to fulfill their purpose. It is this deeper meaning, at both a company level and a personal level, that inspires people to hang together in order to get to results. Let us give you a few examples.

THE MANY WHYS

Over a three-year period, we worked with a twenty-million-dollar, family-owned mining business. Each of those three years, they experienced a 10 percent growth in revenue. The company mines the highest grade of magnesium and makes a darn good profit by partnering with a much larger company that uses magnesium to make high-grade pharmaceuticals. The business is highly profitable. Even so, money is not the only thing that drives the leadership team.

This magnesium mining company is in a beautiful, remote, mountain-range town. People don't have a lot of options for safe, rewarding, well-paying jobs. Their core purpose is *to provide magnesium to the world while supporting the families in our community.*

Another example is a smash-hit, start-up niche distillery that makes innovative spirits. The company was created by a couple after the husband lost his job as a refinery engineer. The pair wanted to stay in their hometown, but finding another job in the area was nearly impossible. The town's largest employer had shut down, and many people lost their jobs. But the husband had a talent for building distillery equipment and had a passion for making spirits.

Together they decided to launch a company that would take advantage of those skills and center it around their local community, which had once been strong. When we worked with them, their core purpose was clear: *to provide an impactful return on community, telling stories of our past and writing new chapters for our future.* The town could enthusiastically rally around the story and inspiration behind the distillery.

Both of these organizations knew their big *why*—their mission statement, their purpose for existing. Both companies are financially successful, but their purposes have a strong community focus.

Why are these *whys* so impactful? A company *why* is like a romance. Humans thrive on romance or falling in love.

When you are courting your potential mate, there is a drive to connect. This drive is created in part by the release of a hormone that acts like a drug in the brain. The same is true with a newborn baby or puppy. Those strong feelings of responsibility and somewhat blinding loyalty establish a connection that is strong even in the face of challenge and turbulence.

When we first fall in love, we project our hopes and dreams onto the person we adore. We believe that person to be *my prince charming,* or *the love of my life.* We feel certain that our newborn child will be brilliant and wildly successful! We project our expectations onto the other without really knowing yet who they are. Those hopes and dreams give us tremendous energy and drive to engage with the other and plan a life together.

The same is true within a company. The vision (the *why*) ignites and pulls people in, and it pulls on the emotions of everyone who is engaged. Once people are pulled in, the big *why* must sustain the individual within the relationship through the growing stages and development of the business or project.

THE PERSONAL WHY

The hope is that each person who comes to work for your company is inspired by your big *corporate why*, and that *why* trickles down to employees on an individual level. The power of the team increases when each person in the company, team, or project also has her own personal skin in the game—her personal *why*. She needs to know what's in it for her, "Why does this matter to me personally?"

This is especially critical for the millennial generation in the work force. Unlike those who came before, millennials are not willing to blindly do their time, climb the ladder, and get the promotion. They must have personal meaning and purpose to stay engaged.

When each individual connects her personal *why* to the big *why*, the group harnesses a free natural resource: inspiration that carries the person, the team, and the organization through tough times and conflict. The big *why* ignites people's commitment. The personal *why* sustains it.

My (CrisMarie's) personal *why* is: *to experience the sovereignty that comes when I access my courage and dare to disagree even in the face of someone's authority and/or reaction, and the satisfaction from empowering others to do the same.*

Susan's personal *why* is: *to show up real, raw, and curious about myself and others, embrace and utilize our differences for transformation, creativity, and connection and encourage others to do the same.*

Engaging the personal *why* is one of the greatest challenges in a family-owned business. The founder of a family business usually holds the compelling *why* beyond making money. Part of his *why* may be to have a business that lasts beyond his generation. The incoming generation, on the other hand, may not share that passion or even be interested in carrying on what Dad or Mom started.

If the *why* of the next generation doesn't naturally match the *why* of the parents, a family business will lose its compelling purpose as time goes on. Worst-case scenario, the new generation runs the business into the ground. For a family business to succeed, it must bridge the differences between what made the business great in the beginning and what will make it great going forward.

When we work with teams—corporate, family businesses, non-profits, or start-ups—we begin with ME and WE team focus and then turn toward the business to address some key questions. We ask the group to consider, "Why do we (company or team) exist beyond making money?" The discussion that follows provides great insight into how aligned the team is about the vision and purpose.

We keep it alive by asking, "Why does this matter to each of you personally?" We take time to discover and discuss the personal *why* for the people on the team. Here are some other good questions to ask:

- What draws each of you here?
- What will motivate you when the going gets tough?
- What keeps you here?

Individual connections to the big *why* will pave the way for each individual to show up as the ME, a whole person. If a leadership team, department, and company as a whole doesn't understand and value each person's individual *why* and how that connects them to the bigger *why*, people come to believe that they are expendable, like an object to be used up and thrown away. Objects may be easier to deal with in the beginning, but if people remain objects, they have no motivation to hang in when times get tough or when big change is needed. Objects aren't creative; whole people are creative.

Engaging and nurturing the personal *why* keeps the team connected and engaged. It brings to light when someone is misaligned, however justifiably. Take the time to make sure people are clear on the big *why*, and regularly discuss and check in about personal *whys*. You will be better prepared to position people and the company for success.

So, why does your company or team exist beyond making money? The answer is important for your team, whether you're part of an executive leadership team or on a specific departmental or project team.

Start with why. Make sure everyone knows why this business or project matters beyond making money. Awareness of big *why*, or core purpose, guides your action. Regularly refresh your focus and connection with the big *why*, the real reason you choose to do what you do.

Make sure your big *why* translates down to your personal *why*. Take the time to move beyond a big idea or romance. Sustain your vision by empowering your people to show up as whole people, not mere pieces on the chessboard to be moved about by others.

Now you know the secret of the *why* beneath the *why*! Next up, ensure that inspiration isn't lost amid day-to-day perspiration.

CHAPTER 24
Get Everyone Rowing in the Same Direction

I, CrisMarie, am an Olympic rower. I know how critical it is for everyone to row well together. It's easy for business leaders to get caught in the tactical, firefighting aspects of day-to-day business and lose the big-picture strategic direction. You busily get things done, but are you moving in the right direction? The opposite also applies: leaders can err on the side of the wider, strategic viewpoint and miss the narrow focus and tactical details required to move the business forward. The big picture is great, but what does it take to make it a reality?

Leaders need crystal clarity to toggle back and forth between a strategic, wide view, and a tactical, narrow focus. Leaders tend to be better in one of these areas than the other. They start off giving great direction, and then fail to check in with their people to see if the direction—both short and long—really is on target.

Regular check-ins on both your wide view and narrow focus ensures you don't miss your ultimate goal. In this chapter, we'll pose some key questions—both wide and narrow—that will help you get to clarity and innovative ideas to provide you with profitable results.

TACTICAL VERSUS STRATEGIC

Leaders, we'd like you to step into an arena with a horse to appreciate the difference between wide view and narrow focus. No, you're not riding the horse. In fact, the horse isn't even wearing a halter. You're on the ground, and you have only one communication tool, a rope in your hands that is not connected to the horse. In the arena, it's your job to navigate the horse through various obstacles. Sound familiar?

The horse is free to comply or not. There's no halter for control, nor is there any incentive. As you can imagine, this situation is loaded with nonverbal cues that interrupt clear communication.

My (Susan's) experiences with this exercise reveal my tendency to quickly narrow my focus. I make a decision to move the horse through a particular obstacle, and if my plan works, I'm satisfied. However, if the horse doesn't play the way I anticipate, I get caught up in a power struggle with the horse. I keep going after the same obstacle and applying more pressure.

To lead more effectively, I need to step back and take a wider view. With a wider viewpoint, I can pick up on the cues from the horse. Some horses are very sensitive, and when I wave the rope up and down in my hands, they instantly react by moving away from me and the motion of the rope. Other horses are less sensitive and more determined to get what they want. These horses easily ignore my waving rope and instead go stand by the side of the arena where there is an open window to the outside.

When I see from a wider view, I am more aware of my own energy. Am I nervous, tight, or anxious? My feeling is communicated to the horse no matter how well I think I'm covering it up.

During our off-site work with clients, we take teams through a series of crucial questions, starting with a wide-view, strategic direction and then moving to a narrow, tactical focus. Wide view gives big-picture direction; narrow focus puts that big picture into action day to day.

Many organizational leaders spend time and energy on developing their vision and mission statements. But when we ask them to tell us their mission statement, they need to pull it out to read it. It's not engrained.

Our goal is to help the leadership team access short, simple answers to these wide-view, strategic questions that are easy to remember because they fit so clearly. When a leadership team can say at the drop of a hat why they exist beyond making money—when it really rings true—we have struck gold. They'll be fully able to drive that clarity down throughout the organization.

Nothing creates alignment better than a team of leaders who all cite the same message and mean it! Your people, your partners, and your clients or customers will believe it and rely on you for it!

WIDE-VIEW QUESTIONS: SETTING STRATEGY

Management consulting experts agree that the key to setting strategy and getting everyone to *row together* is to get clear on three things: your business's or team's:

- core purpose
- core behavioral values (sometimes called *norms*)
- way to define the playing field you're doing business on, your key strategic direction

HOW to get to this clarity is where the management consulting experts differ, and there are lots of different models out there. From all our work, study, and experience, we like Pat Lencioni's six critical questions in his book *The Advantage.*[16] These questions are great at getting to the wide strategic view quickly. We were fortunate to work with Pat for eight years at the Table Group and we think his book, *The Advantage*, may be the best resource for starting with a wide view and driving to a narrow focus.

Here are four of Pat's questions:

1. Why do we exist? (This identifies the core purpose.)
2. How do we behave? (This encapsulates the core behavioral values or team norms.)
3. What do we do? (This defines the concrete business you're in.)
4. How will we succeed? (This identifies three strategic anchors that guide all decision making.)
5. We also add a fifth question: Who do we serve? (This identifies your target market.)

We may not use all questions with every team, but our sweet spot is to use a combination of these questions to help leaders and teams apply the energy of conflict as the secret sauce to turn a great vision into a reality. We bring these questions in after focusing on the ME and WE to ensure that the team engages in healthy conflict during the discussion and arrives at the best answers. Time and time again, we see teams discover answers more quickly when they have done their ME and WE pre-work.

How can you specifically use the wide-view questions? For the first question, "Why do we exist?" you can:

- Ask each team member to jot down a phrase that summarizes why they think the company or team exists.
- Have each person read his statement aloud, with the leader going last. You will have a sense if people are aligned or not, but it is good to make it explicit.
- Ask, "Are we directionally aligned?" Have each person give a quick explicit indicator of if they agree or not. Don't use head nods. Make it more explicit like thumbs up or thumbs down. If not everyone is thumbs up, then it's an indicator for discussion.

Often, one of the four questions requires a deeper dive. Let's explore how we worked with one executive team around the question, "How will we succeed?" We'll look at how they used the strategic anchors on an ongoing basis to drive growth.

Strategic Anchors: How Will We Succeed?

One of our long-term clients was a multi-billion-dollar, multi-national mining company that specialized in precious metals such as copper and gold. When we began working with the company, they were a lower-tier in the industry with a five-person executive team.

The four wide-view questions brought the team to the big why: *to show the world how it is done!* They also got clear on question two, "How will we behave?" They had identified their core behavioral values: *bold and decisive, forthright,* and *adaptable.* Since they were a public company, the answer for, "Who do we serve?" could have simply been their stakeholders or the copper buyers, but that didn't capture their impact. This leadership team also cared about, and knew they couldn't be successful unless they focused on, their impact on the countries where their mines were located. *We serve our stakeholders and the political, labor, and environmental needs of our mines' countries.*

Conflict and misalignment came up when we asked, "How will you succeed?" Some people focused on immediate success, while others took a longer-term view.

We hashed through the state of their business. They had problems with some of the mine sites in countries that were politically unstable. Some of their mine sites were inefficient in finding the metal deposits they needed to meet production levels. What they did agree on was that they wanted to grow, but how?

Reflecting back on what we heard, we asked, "What are you exceptional at?" The answer was unanimous: finding and making successful acquisitions. As a result, *Growth through mergers and acquisitions* became their first strategic anchor.

We carried on by asking, "What else do you need in order to grow?" A discussion ensued on the different mine sites they had acquired. They discovered that they were more successful with mine sites in countries with low political risk than in countries that were unstable. *Low political risk* became the second anchor for growth.

Finally, they realized that in order to be successful, they needed to be operationally efficient, and they struggled with that. They needed to be better at finding the metal deposits. *Geological science* became the final strategic anchor.

By the end of the discussion, the team realized they had significant work to do on the last anchor. When we came back for the next quarterly off-site, they had set their sights on merging with a smaller company that specialized in geological science. This decision was driven by two of their strategic anchors.

The merger went through that year, and we helped them integrate the new company. As with all new relationships, there was conflict of styles and goals, and they added four new leaders to the executive team. When you add even one person to a team, the whole dynamic shifts. We worked with the new team on both the ME (helping people understand their individual styles and impact to their teammates) and the WE (learning to Check It Out! during heated discussions).

Most of the team worked well together, but one team member had repeated run-ins with his teammates. He would agree to a plan of action and then do something different. We helped the team to clear up these differences, and we coached that team member individually. It became clear that he wanted a faster trajectory in his career. He wound up leaving the company.

After he left, the team clicked, things smoothed out, and the company emerged as a mid-tier player in the industry. We re-checked the four wide-view questions with the new team, and they had some heated discussions. They made minor tweaks to the definition of core values, but all in all, the wide-view clarity remained intact.

After the merger, the team commented on how the key to success was getting clear on the strategic anchors. Going through the four questions and diving deeper as needed helped the team shift from random decision making (what seemed good at the time) to focused decision making to drive growth.

Aligning the leadership team around the wide-view questions made for big-picture clarity. That set the direction and priorities, and it simplified decision making for the leadership team and the company. Because they had taken the time to build the ME and the WE their clarity came quickly.

Use this wide-view clarity to drive your monthly and quarterly strategic meetings, and then step back each year to see if it remains accurate. Getting clarity; and, more importantly, maintaining that clarity and alignment around the wide-view questions, sets the direction, defines the game you're playing, and how to move the business forward. Build the ME and the WE so that your wide-view discussions are on the right level and your conversations are real.

NARROW-FOCUS QUESTIONS: DRIVING ACTION

Narrow-focus questions help you bring that big picture strategy into action on a day-to-day basis. The key here, experts agree, is clarifying your team's common goal, getting clear on who's doing what, and having efficient communication. Again, of all the models out there, we like Pat's six critical questions best from *The Advantage*[17], and use the last two for getting to the heart of things quickly/clarifying the nitty/gritty succinctly:

Here are Pat's other two questions:

1. What's most important, right now? (This gets to the heart of the team's collective goal or rally cry.)
2. Who must do what? (This defines roles and responsibilities.)

3. We also add: Who needs to know what? (This clarifies what you need to communicate out.)

These questions are more tactical than the wide-view questions. The answers become the ongoing focus in the short-term. We'll focus on the first narrow-focus question here.

The biggest challenge we find on teams around narrow-focus work is that people tend to center on their own areas. They maximize the success of their departments or silos to the detriment of the business as a whole. When people don't know what's most important at an organizational level, they focus on what they know how to do, which are their areas of responsibility. Your job as a leader is to drive the team to focus collectively. That sets the priorities for the organization and provides the collective focus needed to break down the silos between different departments.

Many companies have annual goals. The trouble is that people tend to forget annual goals until the last half of the year because there is no urgency. Timeframe is important. A shorter timeframe forces the sense of urgency, which helps people work together to accomplish the goal. Make the time-horizon nine, six, or three months, depending upon the size of the goal.

Identify your team's collective goal or rally cry by asking, "What is the most important thing we need to accomplish in the next three to nine months to move our business forward?"

Focusing on short-term immediate needs helps teams to organize and align around what is most important. It ensures all members focus on a collective goal rather than just their own individual area. It's the leader's job to provide clear, long-term and short-term focus so people can stay engaged.

Collective Goal (Rally Cry): What's Most Important, Right Now?

We worked with a niche-player pharmaceutical company known for its expertise in research. The company had three primary departments: research, development, and commercialization, with research being the largest. We were brought in to help them improve the cross-functional teamwork on the project teams working with different drugs. The teams began operating significantly better, and the executive team asked us to conduct their executive off-sites.

The company faced the long-term challenge of bringing its first drug all the way through the process to commercialization. We introduced to the executive team the idea of a rally cry to focus the team as well as the entire company. The executive team knew their long-term company success depended upon successfully submitting their New Drug Application (NDA) and receiving approval by the US Food and Drug Administration (FDA). Their rally cry became: *successful New Drug Application to FDA.* Their advancing objectives included: complete clinical trials; build NDA cross-functional team; write draft NDA application; conduct review cycle; and complete and submit final NDA. These tasks involved only a small subset of the company, but clearly communicating the advancing objectives to the entire company set the priorities for the whole organization.

During the nine months this goal was in place, we worked in the research department with a leader and his team for a two-day off-site. When one of his team members got a call that she was needed at an emergency NDA meeting, there was no question she had to go because the organization's priorities were clear.

As we continued our work for the rest of this three-year engagement, we were impressed with how well the company applied the rally cry tool. A new one was created every six to nine months. Our client learned the importance of defining a collective goal and then advancing objectives.

The client ensured people were clear and emotionally connected to what was most important to move the company forward. This kept the leaders playing together and being accountable for more than just their functional areas.

Leaders and teams tend to narrow in on roles, responsibilities, and processes to deal with setting priorities. But usually that is not the real root of the problem. Once a team achieves the right level of dialogue and conflict, has a wide-focus map that is regularly tested for alignment, and develops a rally cry that gives people a reason to play together, they are clearer on the other two narrow-focus questions.

EMBODY THE BUSINESS

How do you succeed as a leader in conjunction with the business? First, be sure you communicate congruently. Make your words and actions match your inner intent and the core values you have set for your organization. This builds loyalty, and your people will better hear, believe, understand, and act on your message.

Second, toggle between a wide view and a narrow focus depending on the needs of the situation, team, and organization. Both wide-view and narrow-focus questions provide a simple structure that ensures clarity on a team and in an organization. Once you have a clear road map that outlines the answers to these questions, it's crucial to check in regularly. We suggest the following team check-in frequency:

- Weekly check-in: narrow-focus areas
- Monthly check-in: wide-view and narrow-focus areas
- Quarterly check-in: wide-view areas
- Annul check-in: wide-view areas recheck

A great resource on meetings is *Death by Meeting*[18] by Patrick Lencioni. Like horses, your people give cues and feedback as to how effectively you move between a wide and narrow focus. Are you picking up on these cues?

Even if you take care of your wide and narrow focus, you, as a leader, may be making critical mistakes that are undermining your team's success. Read on to find out the five common mistakes leaders make and how to fix them.

CHAPTER 25
Five Mistakes That Stall Your Team and What to Do About Them

Good leaders make basic mistakes that undermine their team's forward progress and stall the business. In this chapter you'll learn five common mistakes leaders make and some simple, practical tools that you can wield immediately to move the team forward and get the business back on track.

Listen in to the leadership team of a manufacturing company at their monthly strategic meeting.

Fritz, the Chief Marketing Officer, says passionately, "We need to put our energy into positioning our new product line and stop spending so much time and focus on the legacy products."

"I totally disagree!" Stanley, Chief of Operations, jumps in. "We need to make sure we don't lose the customers that got us here while we're inventing something new."

Fritz counters, "We definitely need new products."

Betsy, the CFO, laments to Michael, the CEO, "Fritz and Stanley may both be right. We won't know until we do a detailed analysis."

"Okay, okay," Michael concedes. "Fritz and Stanley, you two take your feud offline. We don't have time to do a detailed analysis. We need to make a decision by the end of the week. If you don't come to a solution, I will."

Fritz and Stanley never come to a solution. In the next meeting, Michael lays out the product strategy plan that maintains focus on the existing customer base. Surprised that Michael made a decision without a discussion, the team listens quietly at the table, nodding their heads. Michael interprets these head nods as agreement and commitment.

Michael made several mistakes in this scenario. Do you know what they are?

FIRST MISTAKE: TAKING IT OFFLINE

There are a number of reasons taking something offline is not a good idea. There's no argument that it's appealing and, at first blush, seems efficient. No one wants to sit and listen to two people go back and forth for the umpteenth time.

Teams stuck in this back and forth are missing the point. They're fighting over how to do something (the strategy) because they've lost sight of what problem they want to solve and why (the higher purpose). Let's be clear here: this is a leader and team problem, not just an issue of the two members who are fighting.

So, why not take it offline and come back? Here are our thoughts.

First, the people on your team probably won't take the disagreement offline, just like they didn't in this story. Even if Fritz and Stanley did take it offline, without some accountability and support to have the right conversation, it is unlikely they would actually listen and consider each other's position.

Even when people *do* take the discussion offline and work it out, they often don't let anyone else on the team know. They move on and assume everyone else has too, or it seems redundant to bring it up again. It simply goes quiet. The rest of the team is left wondering: Did they work it out? What was the outcome?

Second, taking something offline limits the shared knowledge of the entire team. Debating in the meeting allows more people to weigh in, ask questions, and build on the ideas of the two people stuck in their positions. This is when a team's creativity and innovation accelerate.

Tool: Treat Your Team Meeting as Your Playing Field

Think of the team meeting as your playing field. It's where you play the game of business. The game doesn't happen during practice or off the field in a solitary cubicle. You win or lose by how you play on the field! For a team to be smarter and more innovative, the entire team needs to be on the field playing the game in the meeting.

SECOND MISTAKE: FOCUSING ONLY ON SOLVING THE BUSINESS PROBLEM

You will reach the best, most creative business solution by being aware of both the ME and WE. It's not enough to focus on solving the business problem without understanding the underlying breakdown in relational health on the team.

Michael, the CEO in our example above, has clearly not addressed the repeating dynamics between Fritz and Stanley. He is so uncomfortable with the tension that he curtails the discussion in order to reach a business solution, albeit his own opinion. He contributes to the logjam by his avoidance.

It's easy to see the business issue as most important. But if you don't address the relational health aspects by having people show up fully, the end solution may be determined by the loudest person or by you alone. A racecar needs to slow down around the curves so it can speed up on the straightaway. In that same way, a leader needs to first ensure the health of the ME and the WE in order to dive deep into clarity.

Tool: Why is This Important to You?

When two approaches to a business scenario are mutually exclusive or irreconcilable, rushing to a solution doesn't work. You wind up solving the wrong problem for the wrong reason. Instead, do some WE work and wade into the tension. Seek to understand where each of these passionate opinions is coming from.

Here's a powerful question to unearth what drives each person, *"Why is this so important to you?"*

Each person's answer will reveal the source of her passion, what drives her from inside. This valuable insight helps you and the team expand your thinking. No longer do you see A versus B. Now you see deeply into the entire scope of the scenario. Asking this question gets you out of either-or thinking and shifts you into the *Aha!* zone of creative solution and innovative problem solving.

Michael could have asked this question of both Fritz and Stanley to get underneath their strong opinions. Instead, he bypassed each of them, and even Betsy, to reach his own solution. His solution clearly was not informed by any of his team's perspectives, and that limited depth, innovation, and buy-in by the team.

THIRD MISTAKE: ASSUMING HEAD NODS MEAN YES

Let's assume the team meets for a third time. This time, Betsy speaks up. "I'm not sure we're going in the right direction. Can we revisit the decision on product strategy?"

How many times has that happened to you? You think the direction is set, only to be revisiting the issue the following week or month.

When Michael had his second meeting, he assumed head nods indicated agreement. More often, head nods mean, "I hear you," or "I'm thinking about what you're saying." They can even mean, "Yeah, and I totally disagree, but I'm not going to say anything right now." Your team deserves a more concrete tool to gauge how people think and feel about a decision.

Tool: Quick Explicit Indicator

We mentioned this idea in Chapter 23 talking about Wide-View questions. Have people make their level of buy-in explicit by either using their thumbs or a color card.

- Thumb up or green card: agree
- Thumb sideways or yellow card: need more discussion
- Thumb down or red card: do not agree

If someone gave a yellow, thumb sideways or red, thumbs down, let them speak and be heard. Engage them in the dialogue. They may present a point of view that you want to incorporate or a question you want to address during implementation. Ask them, "What do you need to be all in?"

This is a quick, simple, and powerful way to focus the discussion that will get to clarity around the table. If everyone doesn't get to a green, thumbs up and the decision is to go ahead, ask if they can disagree and commit. We will address that next.

FOURTH MISTAKE: WORKING FOR CONSENSUS

Different opinions about important strategic issues are exactly what generate creative outcomes. Some leaders are under the impression that they have to work to reach consensus about a final outcome. We disagree. You do want the rich passionate debate, and you do want everything out on the table. But you will waste precious time and water down good ideas if you require everyone to agree.

So, what do you do when the team doesn't all agree?

Adults don't need to get their way, but we do want to feel that we are heard and our ideas are considered. Once that happens—really happens—we can, and will, agree to commit, even if our opinion is different. (For a refresher on effective listening, reread Chapter 21, "Increase Your Team's IQ".)

Tool: Disagree and Commit

Andy Groves, the founder and CEO of Intel, coined the term *disagree and commit*.[19]

When an individual voices her perspective and feels genuinely heard and then commits, even if she still disagrees, she walks out of the meeting with words and actions in alignment with the decision of the team. No one outside that room will know that she had a different opinion.

With this tool we ask the team, "Can you commit to this decision even if you disagree?" and we use the thumbs indicator tool. If thumbs are sideways or down we ask, "What do you need to know, discuss, or have in order to commit?"

Standing behind *disagree and commit* builds team trust and alignment for the decision that carries throughout the rest of the organization because every leader supports the decision by her words and actions.

Imagine after the second meeting if Fritz, who wants to launch the new product line, goes back to his departmental marketing team and says, "Well, I don't agree with Michael's decision. He's making us focus on an existing customer base. I think it's a big mistake!" That statement will destroy the trust, alignment, and cohesion on the leadership team, on his own team and also with people lower in the organization. People will worry and think, "Oh, no! There is chaos up there. Who's running this ship?"

Nothing hinders team cohesion, fractures organizational trust, and causes massive issues more than one person on the leadership team talking behind the team's back. "Well I don't agree, but they're making us do this." That statement infects a deadly corporate cancer. Instead, disagree and commit.

FIFTH MISTAKE: ANALYSIS PARALYSIS

Following the above example, pretend that Michael uses the thumbs indicator in his forth meeting, and it is Betsy who again speaks up. "I'm just not sure we have enough data to be successful."

This is a common reason for a thumb either down or sideways. Don't fear the analyzer, and don't let her stop your team! There's a difference between clarity and certainty. You want clarity, a good direction, and alignment, not perfection. As Colin Powell put it, "Once the information is in the 40 to 70 range, go with your gut."[20] We agree. Don't wait until you can be 100-percent sure, because by then, it's too late.

Procrastination in the name of reducing risk often increases risk because windows of opportunity close. Once you take action, even imperfect action (the dreaded mistake), more relevant data will be revealed to help you find the best path through. A good team can recover from this scenario together.

Tool: Worst Case Scenario

People want certainty when they lack trust in the team's ability to succeed. No matter the reason, a way through this potential blockage is to ask, "What's the worst case scenario?"

When we think through the worst case scenario and believe we can handle it, we open the way to move forward with a *good enough* plan versus a perfect plan. A healthy team that takes imperfect action develops the ability to self-correct.

RECAP

Keep the team moving forward and the Business on track by avoiding these five mistakes:

1. Taking it offline
2. Focusing on solving only the business problem
3. Working for consensus
4. Assuming head nods mean yes
5. Analysis paralysis

Instead, use the five tools to drive great team discussions:

1. Treat the team meeting as your playing field.
2. Ask, "Why is this so important to you?"
3. Use a thumbs or color indicator as a temperature gauge.
4. Request *disagree and commit.*
5. Ask, "What is the worst case scenario?"

These five tools will make you a more effective leader, keep the WE aligned, and keep the business focused on solving the right problems innovatively. Want your teammates to use tools to make your meetings successful? Download *Make Your Meetings Matter* at www.Thriveinc. com/beautyofconflict/bonus.

Is your team the right size? Read on to find out.

CHAPTER 26
Forming the Perfect-Sized Team

When it comes to teams, size matters. We've worked with teams of all sizes, from three to twenty-five members. The right-sized team has between five and twelve members. Jeff Bezos, CEO of Amazon, put it best when he coined the *two pizza rule*[21]: a meeting shouldn't have more people than two pizzas can feed.

Why? A team with fewer than five members lacks the necessary diversity to represent the organization. A team with more than twelve people is cumbersome in dialogue and debate. In large groups, people spend more time reporting on status or advocating for their opinions because they want to be heard. This leaves little room to inquire about each other's ideas. And because the audience is large, team members are more focused on looking smart and are less likely to be vulnerable and ask questions.

The right team size fosters the rich dialogue necessary to discover new possibilities.

Getting the right team size can be a tough pill to swallow for the leader.

Most teams are too big, and leaders don't want to reduce the size for two reasons:

1. They have strong performers whose input they want and worry it won't happen if they aren't at the table.
2. People are fighting to be on the team because they want the ear of the leader.

Neither of these reasons merits keeping a large leadership team. Both reasons reflect a different problem; primarily, lack of good regular back-and-forth communication.

Most people fight to be at the leadership table because they are concerned they won't get the right information, or their concerns won't be heard unless they are present. When that issue is clearly dealt with by an effective flow of information, people are generally quite happy to let go of the leadership table and focus on the work that needs to be done.

One of the main jobs of a team member is to communicate leadership-team information to their own direct reports. It requires discipline to determine what needs to be communicated to whom at the end of a leadership-team meeting. And it requires commitment by each team member that they will do so quickly, within twenty-four hours, with their teams. This type of disseminating communication is a key discipline that resolves issue of team size.

Each time we have coached a large team, we've had to work diligently to convince the leader to reduce the size. We usually pair this discussion with additional coaching about organizational communication. In all cases, after just a couple months, not only have the leaders been happy and more productive, but so have the folks who were pulled off the team. And guess what? Other employees in the company were happy with the change too. We'll share a client example to illustrate how this works.

DOWNSIZING TECH LEADERSHIP

Early in our business we worked with one team at a technical engineering company. The leader, Fred, a VP, invited us to work with his team of twenty-five. When we asked if his team really had twenty-five members, he explained that only eight reported to him, but if he didn't invite the rest, it would create lots of political issues. We understand that politics is a reality for most corporate cultures. After much dialogue, Fred agreed to reduce the group to eighteen. However, when we showed up for the two-day off-site, there were twenty-one at the table. Somehow he managed to slip three more through the door.

We went forward with the planned off-site. We agreed that the best way to approach this session was to let Fred discover the problem himself.

The first morning of our two-day off-site is designed to help people build trust and goodwill toward each other. We do this to create an atmosphere where people will dive into dialogue and debate about the real-time strategic issues facing the team. The logistics of building trust around the different styles of twenty-one people is challenging, but heck, we could do that. The situation wasn't perfect. In a group that large, people aren't as willing to be real and vulnerable. But it can be done.

The real problem isn't developing trust and fostering goodwill. The real problem shows up once we dive into the business issues.

Sure enough, we got to the business discussion in the afternoon of day one, and things unraveled. As folks discussed the team's direction and what goals were most important, everyone wanted to put in their two cents. No one took the time to ask questions or clarify what someone else said because that would take away from their speaking time. At the end of the first day, we went to dinner with the team. Conversation around the table revealed that people were frustrated and wanted something different. Fred, over a glass of wine, said he thought the team was too big.

The next day, we brought up the idea of shifting the team size. After some discussion, the group agreed the current size wasn't satisfying and that a smaller group would be better. The problem: no one thought they should be the one to leave.

We asked, "Why don't you want to leave?" What came out was that matters discussed at the leadership level rarely disseminated down. Meetings throughout the organization consisted of reporting on status, with very little time spent dialoguing.

We introduced our ideas about disseminating leadership team communication through a rhythm and structure that the next level down could adopt. We suggested ways to improve the meetings and the importance of building in time for debate, as well as specifically clarifying what would be disseminated and what would not.

The group discussed and agreed: The pared-down leadership team and newly structured lower level teams would use both the meeting model and disseminating communication tools. The team agreed to let Fred decide who was the right fit for the leadership team. Fred chose his eight direct reports plus his HR person and him. The new team size was ten.

It didn't go perfectly. We worked with them to tweak things over the next year.

Some people were upset to be left off the team. They felt like they were losing power. They feared they would be marginalized. We worked with the leader and these people to hear and validate their concerns. We asked if they would be willing to test drive the new team structure for ninety days.

A month later we returned and had a great meeting with the pared-down leadership team. They dove in, engaged in healthy conflict, and reached some key decisions. We learned later, though, that while they loved their new leadership team meetings, they had not invested the same effort into the meetings with their direct reports, the people who had been at the previous meeting. Those folks were unhappy. The people who had been asked to leave the team were realizing their worst fears.

The team renewed their commitment to communicate to their own direct reports within twenty-four hours of the leadership meeting. We supported the company rolling out the meeting model based on smaller team sizes and disseminating communication while ensuring leaders were trained to create similar team commitments with their direct reports.

At our second on-site meeting at the ninety-day mark, we learned that they had applied the smaller leadership team size to the next level. The leadership team was not only clearer and more defined, but information disseminated down to those who weren't there in person, and feedback was coming back up. They liked that!

Fred has since moved on to another technical engineering company. Right away he reduced his team size. He now communicates the value of a smaller leadership team and quickly gets the buy-in. But when he invited us in to kick off his new team, he told us there would be eighteen in the room.

We opened our mouths to challenge him, and he laughed. "Got you!" In fact, he had reduced this group size to eight!

As Fred learned, size does indeed matter, but in this case bigger isn't better. Having a team that is willing to inquire, question, and debate is essential. If more people are asking to come to the meeting, it's likely that communication is not flowing into the organization. People aren't getting the information they need. Once you have the right team size, ensure the efficient outflow of communication and inflow of feedback.

When your leadership team is the right size and you are working on the WE, you foster healthy, engaged conflict and clarity on organizational direction, both wide view and narrow focus. Help the rest of the organization stay in step. Build the commitment for team members to quickly and consistently communicate information to those who need it. The organization will be informed and sigh in relief knowing that the leadership team is working together.

Read on to learn how to make your meetings matter.

CHAPTER 27
Make Your Meetings Matter

"We have too many meetings."

"Our meetings are not effective."

"Our meetings are full of boring status reporting."

Sound familiar? If you're like most of the leaders we work with, you've said one or all of these many, many times throughout your career.

Stop complaining! Think of your meetings like an athlete thinks of training for his sport. Anyone who has ever played a team sport knows that you have to *practice together*. As a rower, no amount of time that I, CrisMarie, spent rowing on an ergometer, lifting weights, and running was going to prepare me for a race. I needed time with my teammates in a boat on the water learning how to row together. We had to find our rhythm and learn to work with each other.

The same is true in business. No amount of time spent in your office or cubical designing *your* plan is going to change the business unless you consider your teammates' insights, questions, and input. If you've hired smart, passionate people who are aligned around a collective goal, conflict should happen every time you gather around a table.

239

Meetings are where you get in the boat together. You make time for debate and discussion, and you use the energy of conflict to increase the team's EQ (emotional intelligence) and IQ (intellectual intelligence). That only happens when the team talks together about the business and issues as they come up.

NO WONDER LEADERS COMPLAIN ABOUT MEETINGS

When Susan and I first chat with a leader, we ask, "How often does your team meet together?" We are amazed at how little time the team actually spends together. Sometimes leaders try to manage the team through one-on-ones. Even scheduled team meetings are often canceled.

"We've got too much going on and too many other meetings," they reply. "Plus, I have monthly one-on-ones with everyone." They believe that one-on-one meetings or gathering in small subsets will keep things efficient. Leaders assume that having one-on-ones will make their direct reports more effective at their jobs. While this may help a person in her individual area, it undermines and denies the importance and value of the team.

Teams that do meet together regularly usually do so weekly. When we ask how those meetings are going, they respond, "Well, everyone goes around and reports the status on their area. Actually, it can be pretty boring and not very engaging." No wonder business leaders complain about their meetings!

The problem isn't the meeting. The problem is the way the meeting is run.

Teams are a collection of diverse people. The benefit of a team is in the collective brainpower of an entire group. But if that group doesn't interact or take time to learn and appreciate the power of the team, it's like playing basketball with a team of great shooters who can't pass the ball or run a play together.

Effective meetings are often uncomfortable, because tension develops as people throw out different ideas. Instead of status reporting (which we suggest saving for e-mail), discuss the important topics and let your best minds passionately figure out the solution. That puts you smack dab into conflict. And when you lean into that conflict, you get to the gold mine of innovative, creative, and profitable results. When meetings are done right, leaders will see the value of meetings and look forward to them.

THREE TOOLS FOR EFFECTIVE MEETINGS

In rowing, I (CrisMarie) needed to know what to focus on that would most improve my performance. In business, it's important to know how to use conflict in the context of a meeting so that people eagerly engage. Here are three basic tools to help.

1. Team Norms: Rules for the Race

Team norms are not rules. They are a small set of behaviors which, if adhered to, will dramatically improve the WE and the business results. Developing team norms sets the expectations of how to behave in a meeting. Team norms are the rules for the race. To develop your team norms, your group needs to know what its problem areas are and build norms around those issues. In Chapter 20 we talked about five steps to build and use team norms. Now, let's tie them to an example.

Step one: Brainstorm what is and isn't working in your meetings. Use a whiteboard or flip chart. Start first with what works well. Here is how one client did this.

WHAT'S WORKING?	WHAT'S NOT WORKING?
✓ We have a good rhythm for our meetings ✓ Monthly strategic meetings are useful ✓ Our numbers are up ✓ We know our priorities ✓ We get along	○ Roles and responsibilities are not clear ○ People come in late to our meetings ○ We don't each communicate key messages from our team meetings down to our direct reports ○ We do status reporting during our weekly meeting ○ We don't work well across departments

Step two: Discuss the impact these behaviors have on the team. When you take the time to ask, you will discover underlying causes to the behaviors. Ask, "How does this impact the team?" or "Why is this a problem?" This ensures you're solving the right problem.

Step three: Identify the top three problem behaviors which, if shifted, would dramatically improve your meetings and team performance.

We say three because some teams have a long list of norms. Who can remember a long list? Choose only three problems to address. When you find improvement, you can move on to a new set of three. Our client's team decided on the following:

WHAT'S NOT WORKING?
1. We don't all communicate to the next level on time or at all. 2. People come in late to our meetings. 3. We do status reporting during our weekly meeting.

The other two issues—not working well across departments and lacking clear roles and responsibilities—can be discussed and addressed as key strategic topics rather than made into team norms. Team norms are for persistent problem behaviors.

Step four: Turn those problems around to the desired behaviors. At this point, have an open discussion about what might be alternative healthy or productive behaviors. We use a neighboring flip chart so everyone can see both the unproductive and productive behaviors. Here's an example of that same team's ideas for productive behaviors.

WHAT'S NOT WORKING?	TEAM NORMS (WHAT TO DO DIFFERENTLY)
1. We don't all communicate to the next level on time or at all. 2. People come in late to our meetings. 3. We do status reporting during our weekly meeting.	• Commit to communicate within 24 hours. • Be on time. • Bring hot topics to meetings and share status via e-mail (unless urgent).

Step five: Hold your team accountable. When someone doesn't behave in alignment with your team norms, use the model from the WE: *Check It Out!* (Use only data and curiosity). For example, if someone is late to a team meeting, you can say, "I noticed you walked in ten minutes late. [Data] We have a norm that says we'll be on time. [Data] What happened? [Curiosity]"

When the leader holds the team member accountable for the team norm, other people know that working hard to be on time was worth it, and they will keep doing it. This sets the context for people to feel worthy and engaged in a meeting. Make team norms matter. Talk about them, and check it out when someone behaves out of alignment with the team norms.

2. Turn Toward Conflict: Give Permission to Hang In

The fact is that most individuals are not comfortable with conflict. In a meeting people tend to turn away from it, ignore it, pretend it is not happening and carry on. Nothing could be less effective, especially because the people in the conflict—whether it is overt or covert— remain stuck in the conflict and, therefore, can't fully access their creative brains.

As the leader, pay attention to the signs and signals of conflict. For example, someone raises his voice to repeat something or others lean back and look away. When you notice conflict, acknowledge it, check it out, and give the space and permission for people to deal with it. Let people know that conflict is okay, and even expected, and that opting in, hanging in, and working out their differences is powerful, even if it seems counter cultural. Reinforce the behavior by acknowledging *good job,* even if it doesn't go well. This fosters an environment in which people will try it next time.

To reiterate, here are the four steps to turn toward conflict during a meeting:

1. Pay attention to signs and signals that conflict is in the air.
2. Acknowledge what you think is happening and check it out.
3. Give space and permission to opt in, hang in, and work it through.
4. Give them a *good job*, even if it didn't go well.

3. Build on Ideas: Reflect Back What You Are Hearing

We want people to develop skills to build on each other's ideas during conflict, not tear each other apart until the *best* person wins. A helpful tool that works beautifully in tense situations is reflecting back.

Reflect back what you've heard rather than restate your own point in another way. There are three steps for reflecting back:

1. After listening, repeat what you've digested from what the other person said. (Don't just say, "I hear you.")
2. Include what you're picking up emotionally from what they are saying.
3. Ask for confirmation: "Did I get it?" This gives them the space to clarify ideas or concepts if what you heard is not what they meant to say.

For example, "It sounds like you want to take a more conservative approach because you think my idea would threaten our current cash flow, and you're frustrated that I keep bringing this idea up. Did I understand you correctly?"

Bridging differences helps get to innovation and creativity without breaking trust. It includes learning to build on each other's input instead of sticking stubbornly to your own story. It takes listening, reflecting back, and checking it out. For most of us, this is a skill that needs to be developed, as opposed to something we do instinctively.

MEETINGS THAT MATTER

Meetings are where your team plays together. It's where they get work done. Use the tools we covered in this chapter to make your meetings more effective. You can:

Create team norms, so people know the behaviors to avoid and the productive behaviors that are expected.

Follow the four steps to turn toward conflict, so you set the stage for people to follow.

Build on ideas by following the three steps for reflecting back what you heard.

We don't pretend this is easy. It's not. Behaviors lead to results. I (CrisMarie) did not get to the Olympics by being casual and ignoring my alarm at five o'clock every morning. Instead, I got up and worked out twice a day, six days a week, for six years. You can build a strong WE, and your team can produce innovative, profitable results in the business. It takes your commitment and discipline to hold you and your team to these higher standards day in and day out. When you do, your team's ability to play together will skyrocket, as will their competitive advantage. Want your team to know and use these tools? Download *Make Your Meetings Matter* at www.Thriveinc.com/beautyofconflict/bonus.

What do you do when a big change is needed? How do you get people to change? Read on to find out.

CHAPTER 28
Increase Your ROI on Change

Imagine you are leading your organization through a large change project: a merger and acquisition, reorganization, or massive technology project. As the leader, you have worked out the strategic plan, budget, resources, and timeline. All set, right? Wrong.

The Economist's Intelligence Unit, sponsored by The Project Management Institute, conducted a survey in March of 2013 on strategic change project success. These 587 senior executives who were surveyed globally believe the failure rate on *strategic initiatives* is 44 percent.[22] This is extremely high risk. We think that number reflects the fact that leaders aren't focusing on how to help the humans in the organization adopt the change.

You will not reap the ROI on your big change project unless you bring along the people in your organization. Sadly, for many leaders that is often an afterthought. When change occurs, conflict erupts. People don't understand why the organization is changing, or they disagree with the changes. Some individuals don't want to let go of their old ways of doing things. They have a lot at stake.

People resist. Productivity suffers. Morale tanks. ROI is lost.

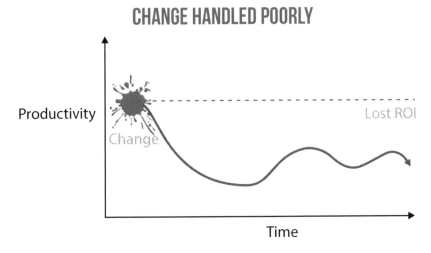

CHANGE HANDLED POORLY

Don't waste your time and money by not proactively considering the human element. Remember, your business is made up of a lot of MEs, individuals who have their own concerns and styles for handling change. When you focus energy on the ME and the WE, business results will increase dramatically.

MONEY DOWN THE DRAIN

When I, CrisMarie, worked at Arthur Andersen, I helped executive teams implement large-scale changes such as mergers, reorganizations, and enterprise resource planning systems. The biggest mistake CEOs made was to focus only on the business or smart side of projects without including the human or healthy side of projects. Ignoring people is like throwing money down the drain.

I came in to help the CEOs repair the damage resulting from a business-only focus. My Arthur Andersen team had one frustrated CEO, Bill, who called us after his company had spent a significant amount of money implementing a new financial system, and the project was failing miserably. Despite his efforts to tell, train, encourage, and force people to use the new system, employees kept their own systems in place, undermining the benefits of an integrated financial system.

In my interviews, I quickly learned that key financial data was missing from the new system. That caused manual workarounds, and it was so complex that it couldn't help people meet their current workload demands, even if it might prove beneficial in the long run. The finance team was mad, even insulted, that Bill had not chosen the system they liked best.

I brought Bill to the financial department with the CFO to hear the frustrations of people in the finance department. It may seem like overkill to engage the CEO at this level, but the finance department had taken the decision quite personally. They wanted to be heard by Bill. He did a good job of reflecting back what he heard, he acknowledged his choice was different from what they wanted, and he expressed his desire to make it work. Good job, Bill!

After listening, he said, "We are going to use this new system, but tell me how we can make it work for you." Together, they came up with a plan, and Bill was committed to making it work.

Bill, with the CFO and the entire finance team, gathered to kick-off a three-day boot camp to focus on three areas: advanced training, missing-data entry, and complex test, simulation, and troubleshooting. During the three days Bill came in and out checking on the progress of the team. At the end of the boot camp, the system was fully operational, and the finance department was its biggest supporter! Clearly, taking the time and effort to communicate, work together, and problem solve key issues was more powerful than giving the team a binder to work through.

WHY, WHAT, HOW, AND WHO

If you want a group or team to buy into a new way of doing something, focus on the human aspect. Get people involved, listen to them, and work together. You will build tremendous loyalty and engagement, and that is priceless. As coaches, our work with leaders includes focusing on the human side, which helps them reap the ROI of their business or smart investment. In short, we teach leaders to be proactive with change.

When I, CrisMarie, was consulting with Blue Cross Blue Shield in the early 2000s, I was lucky enough to get certified in the *Leading and Managing Organizational Transitions* through William Bridges & Associates. Much of how I approach change initiatives is influenced by William Bridges, the grandfather of change management and author of *Managing Transitions*.[23]

A critical proactive measure is to be sure you communicate early, often, and in varied ways. Give your people what they need to get on board with the change. I've adapted Bridges work for this simple communication framework called *why, what, how, and who*. For people to buy in to change, they need to see the change from your point of view. You know *why* you want to change, *what* you are aiming for, *how* you are going to get there, and *who* needs to do what. Map that out for them, and remind them often along the way.

Why Start with why. People need to understand why this change is so important. You have a good reason. Let them know what it is.

What Paint a picture of how the world will look and feel on the other side of the change so people understand what you are aiming for. Your team wants to know how the destination will look and feel. Understanding the target will help them gauge their progress along the way.

How Lay out a step-by-step plan how the organization will get to the final destination. Plans may change as you travel and close the gap between where the organization is now and where you want it to go. Offer frequent updates.

Who Who needs to do what? Help people understand

their role in making this change a reality. You can't do it alone. Giving people a role helps them buy in to the change as they participate in the implementation.

In addition to the why, what, how, and who, people want to know that you care about more than just the business results. They want to know you care about them as human beings. When you communicate, let people feel like they are part of this process, because they are. You literally could not do it without them. Here are two ways to ensure your people stay engaged and on track to integrate the change:

1. Show them they matter as people. They are not just cogs in the wheel. You hear and understand their points of view. Be considerate. Let them talk about where they are in the change process, especially if they are upset with it. Shutting down their frustrations only sends those feelings underground, causing bigger problems.

2. Let them know you haven't discarded them. Show the team how they are still connected to the company, to you, and to each other in the midst of this change. Give them a specific role to play, hear their feedback, and encourage their participation in the solution.

Combine the why, what, how, and who when you address the organization. This detailed communication gives people clarity about where they are going, and helps them get and stay engaged.

What happens when things get bleak? Let's look at the Valley of Despair.

VALLEY OF DESPAIR

Change requires people to work differently, be it on a system or in a specific business process. Going from what was to what will be involves a period of transition. During this transition, productivity almost always drops. In change management circles, this is called the Valley of Despair. It's based on and adapted by various Change Management experts from

Elisabeth Kubler-Ross's "Five Stages of Grief" described in her book, *On Death & Dying.*[24] Productivity drop during transition is due in part to concrete changes such as new systems and processes. It's also due to the internal process human beings navigate to embrace the change.

CHANGE HANDLED WELL

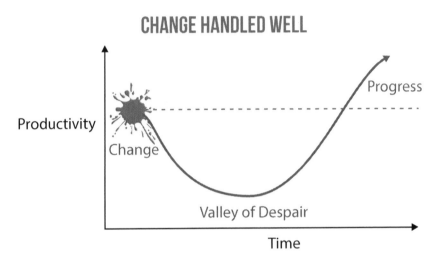

William Bridges says that when change occurs, people have to experience psychological reorientation to the new way of being. For people who have been doing the same things at the same place for a long time, this does not happen overnight. People process at different speeds. As a leader, you can support individuals to move through this process.

What seems like resistance is often fear of the unknown. Most people really do want to do a good job. They resist the new way because they're afraid of losing competency, status, control, relationships, turf, meaning, and/or identity. This fear mires them in resistance. Getting specific about what they fear they are losing and acknowledging that fear will help them move through the resistance.

For example, someone loses his feeling of competency when a new enterprise resource planning system comes in. His feeling is justified because employees are now a beginner in the new system. If they don't acknowledge this loss, they will likely feel threatened, and may even quit.

All their organizational knowledge walks out the door with them. If they first acknowledge the loss, they can then feel it and move through to acceptance that they are a beginner. This makes it easier for them to engage in the training that is offered. Acknowledgement of what is being lost cuts down to size the impact of change. The system is new, but they still know all about the organization.

Once they identify their loss, they can move through the next phase and figure out how to replace or redefine what they have lost. Sometimes they have to come to terms with the need to relinquish something. We've seen this firsthand many times, but one particular client makes for a great case study.

We worked with an international, multi-billion dollar medical supply organization on a merger and acquisition. They were a big, stable, process-oriented sales engine that was acquiring a small, innovative start-up. It was like merging David and Goliath.

The leaders of the start-up, the David, were terrified their culture wouldn't survive the merger with the much larger Goliath. It was easier for Goliath to assume everything would go their way, but they desperately needed to be innovative in order to succeed in their industry. To help these two disparate cultures merge, we developed a cross-company change team with key people from both organizations. We worked with this leadership change team to develop a nexus of trust, communication, purpose, and plan to drive a successful merger. Once the team was clear, aligned, and operating well, we expanded to the next layer in the organization.

We conducted cross-company workshops on change. At these workshops, members from the leadership change team talked about their own experience with the change by discussing what was working and where they were struggling. It was authentic and real. Other leaders from both companies stood together and shared their common goals for the change.

During these interactive workshops, we provided tools and created experiences for the larger group to honestly discuss their views on the change cycle. Many related to being in the Valley of Despair. Asking questions, giving feedback, and checking out their stories of concern helped them digest the change and actively move along the change cycle.

We also taught them skills to deal with differences effectively, since we knew they would keep bumping into conflict throughout the change process. They made cross-company personal connections, which built trust and communication and went a long way toward breaking down the us-versus-them barrier.

In the end, the companies merged successfully and profitably, gaining the ROI they had hoped to achieve. Were there casualties? Yes, as there always are with big change. But the new culture harnessed the innovative nature of David while benefitting from the process-oriented sales expertise of Goliath.

Communication—early and often—is a key responsibility for leaders implementing big change. Communicate *why* the organization is changing, *what* the end goal looks and feels like, *how* they will get there, and *who* will do what to make it so. And remember, success depends on bringing your people along. Treat them as humans so they know they matter to you, to the company, and to each other. Be prepared for the Valley of Despair, and provide a path for individuals to honestly talk about their struggles in the change process. Give them ways to identify what specifically they're losing in this change and how they can replace, redefine, or relinquish what they have lost.

Finally, keep in mind that big change can take months or years to successfully implement. Stay connected to your people for the entire journey.

HOW TO COMMUNICATE CHANGE

You've probably noticed a theme in this chapter on change: communicate. While communication is multifaceted, there are a few key tools to support you in effectively communicating change in your organization. You, the leader, are the marketing arm to the rest of the organization. Pay attention to not only *what* you communicate, but *how* you communicate it.

Here are three common mistakes leaders make in communicating change:

1. Sending crucial information by e-mail. Mistaken belief: Everyone now knows what to do and why. Everything will flow smoothly.

2. Making a binder. In an off-site, the leader and the team create a binder with all the important information. Mistaken belief: Now that it's all decided, everyone will reference the binder and act differently.

3. Being unclear and not taking the time to clarify the change; and therefore, being out of alignment about the why, what, how, and who. Result: each member of the leadership team says something different about what's happening with the change process. This equates to chaos and mistrust.

4. Focusing on the mechanics of the change or the impact to the bottom line without considering the human impact. Result: people feel disregarded and resist.

You're lucky if people open and read the e-mail. And a binder—really? And, when leadership team members tell different versions, people further down the organizational chain talk and compare notes. Distrust grows, and people begin to worry. It's like being in a family: if Mom and Dad contradict each other, the kids manipulate the situation to get their way.

How you communicate is just as important as what you communicate.

You need to make information accessible, understandable, and palatable. Here are four ways to effectively communicate:

1. As a leadership team, make sure you are clear and aligned about the why, what, how, and who of the change. Then at the end of each leadership team meeting, identify exactly what you want people in the organization to know, versus what you want to keep within the leadership-team cone of confidentiality.

2. Use the rumor mill. Every organization has break-room gossip, so why not use it? Once you have clarity on what to communicate, each leadership team member can actively communicate that message to his team. This works best if it happens face-to-face within twenty-four hours. If your business model doesn't allow for that, do the best you can.

3. Repeat the message in different venues, such as all-hands meetings, in company newsletters, or at social events such as picnics. It's normal to assume that if you say something once, people will understand and just do it. But as in marketing, you need to communicate your key change messages six or seven times before people will pay attention to you, hear you, believe you, understand you, know how to behave differently, and change their behavior. Six or seven times! That's a lot of repetition, but that's what it takes.

4. Tell stories. Humans absorb, learn, and are changed through story telling. Your people will learn more easily if you tell a story that depicts what it takes to make the change work, or if you share the impact this change will have, or has had, on a customer.

For example, if a consumer products company's leadership team decided to change their target market and marketing strategies for one of their primary products, you might first think, "Just inform the marketing team." But if that happened, marketing would make the changes, and people in other departments wouldn't know why. People throughout the organization would wonder, worry, and make stuff up. The leadership team would appear not to know what they're doing, or that they are working against each other.

Organizational communication needs to be broader and more integrated and led by each team member. It must be done over and over again, telling stories about why, and what it will look like when it's done, how the company will get there and what role you want them to play.

When each member of leadership takes the time to communicate the appropriate changes to his team, everyone in the organization is on the same page. Issues surface and are addressed, and the leadership team looks to be in alignment, because they are! The company breathes a collective sigh of relief.

Change is hard. It is even harder when it feels like it is being done to you, and for many people in an organization that's how it is taken. You, the leader, are way out in front of this change process, like the fastest runner in a marathon who is almost 20 percent done with the race when other people are just starting the race. You need to help your people move through the Valley of Despair. You and your leadership team need to be master communicators and story tellers to help your people become aware, digest, adopt, and in the best case, embrace the change. Remember, these are humans who are accustomed to doing things the old way. Let them know that you care and that they matter by supporting them through the change.

Did we mention that you have to repeat yourself?

Want to hear how big and small companies used the Path to Collective Creativity model to get to collective results? Read on.

CHAPTER 29
Transform Your Team from Conflict to Brilliance

In an effort to improve our own marketing, we hear from well-meaning colleagues and friends who advise us to focus our work on a particular industry or size of company. We have resisted this advice, finding success in the work we do across all types and sizes of businesses.

This is no surprise to us, since businesses, large and small, that make up technology, consumer products, medical, manufacturing, pharmaceutical, and other services are all made up of people working in teams. Teams can't work without repeated conflict. How we choose to deal with that conflict—avoid it or use it—makes the difference between success and failure in that situation and, ultimately, in the company.

To this point, we'll share two client examples where big bottom-line impacts and seemingly irreconcilable differences led to co-creative outcomes when these very different leadership teams chose to use the conflict.

FROM BIG DATA TO BIG RESULTS

We worked with a computer analytics company whose revenue was more than $200 million in the year we started with them. The company specialized in analyzing large data sets. For this story, we'll refer to them as CAC (Computer Analytics Company). Our initial focus was to develop a stronger, aligned leadership team with a clear strategy.

The company was solid and doing well in its main business line of providing data analytical solutions, but in our work together, the leadership team realized they did not have a strong growth plan. With the analytics industry heating up, the company needed to stay ahead of the game and develop some commercial data analytic tools.

Six months into our two-year engagement, CAC added Bob, VP of Business Development. Bob's focus was on developing new product lines, which he had done successfully at other companies. Bob jumped right into the team discussions, providing a unique point of view that the team seemed to need and value. He had been assigned the task of focusing on building the new business lines in commercial analytics, which would create a completely different type of business.

Fast forward another six months. In preparation for the annual two-day off-site, we discussed the agenda with Mike, the CEO. Mike was upset. In prepping for the off-site, he had reviewed the financials and discovered a $500,000 expense that didn't make sense to him. He saw it as a sign that the team was slipping in terms of communication, alignment, and accountability. He wanted to address these issues.

While we appreciated the heads up, we suggested that Mike not make this the first agenda item since he probably wouldn't get the best dialogue from his team. But when we kicked off the first meeting, Mike dove right in.

"Hey, what the heck is going on," he burst out. "We have a $500,000 unexplained expense that I want to get to the bottom of!"

Bob spoke right up. "I can explain it," he said. "You told me to get the new business line up and running. I went looking for in-house resources, but Maggie wasn't able to provide any. So I did what I had to do and hired outside consultants. I'd say, six months—well, that is most of the $500,000."

Before Mike could say anything, Maggie, the COO and the one responsible for the bulk of CAC's revenue and engineers, jumped in. "Look, you're not going to blame me for this, Bob," she said. "You came to me with some half-baked plan. No way was I going to take my engineers away from real business to do something like that."

Mike was peeved. "Come on, you guys! What the hell? Couldn't you have worked this out?"

"Well, Mike, you were clear. You said, 'Get it done.' And I did, didn't I?" Bob obviously didn't see the problem.

"Look, Mike, he came to me once, and what he presented was *not* a plan!" Maggie was quite sure she had done the right thing to protect CAC.

You probably recognize this as a classic case of opting out of the tension of an oh, sh*t! moment.

Because we had been working with the team for some time, we arranged this off-site to be at a ranch in Montana where the team could work with horses. We could see that the $500,000 was only the surface issue— the deeper issue was team dynamics. We requested that the team hold off trying to resolve the issue. The problem had been building for six months. We wanted to offer the team some ME and WE time with the horses, so they could engage in the right business conversation instead of just solving a problem.

The team, trusting us and the process, agreed.

We brought the group to an arena filled with a series of obstacles. We brought three horses into the arena and let them run free. Then we asked for three volunteers to come into the arena. The goal was to successfully work as a team to move the horses through the obstacles. The catch: there could be no verbal communication.

Guess who volunteered first? Mike, Bob, and Maggie.

Bob moved in quickly and was clearly comfortable around horses. He walked toward the horses with authority, and they moved quickly toward the other end of the arena. Mike walked toward Bob and the horses. Maggie stepped into the arena and pressed herself against the gate, not taking one step toward the animals.

Bob continued driving, and the horses responded with speed. But it was clear that the horses felt pressured. As soon as the horses reached the far end, all three turned quickly and headed straight for Maggie!

Mike stepped back toward Maggie, making himself big, and the horses veered away. The horses wound up in a corner as far away as they could get from all three humans. We asked for a time out and debrief with Mike, Bob, and Maggie.

Bob spoke first, clearly frustrated. "I can't believe it! Where were you guys? I was doing all the work with no support!"

Mike and Maggie were silent.

Susan asked Bob, "I get that you had a plan and some horse whispering skills, but I'm wondering: were you aware of your teammates?"

"It's just that they weren't any help to me!" he said.

Susan continued, "Okay, why don't you find out about them now."

Bob paused. Finally, he asked, "Mike, Maggie, what happened? Why weren't you helping me?"

Maggie spoke first, her voice tight and angry. "Well, geez, I'm not a horse person. They're big animals that move fast. I wasn't about to follow you. Besides, I had no idea what you had in mind!"

Mike chimed in, "Look, Bob, I saw that you had something in mind, but I wasn't sure what. Then I noticed Maggie wasn't with us. I was definitely torn." He looked reflective. "That's how I often feel when you guys, well any of you…" (he looked back at the rest of the team outside the arena) "are off doing your thing but not working together."

Another team member spoke up. "I have to say, what just happened in the arena is definitely what happens with you three in the office, and maybe also for more of us. But wow! It was so obvious to watch it play out!"

"Well, I do like to make things happen," Bob said. "I guess my Superstar style overrules when it comes to me working with the team. If I hit any resistance with anyone, I just think, *I'll do it myself.*"

"Look, I'm risk averse. This is just how I am," Maggie responded. "I get that sometimes I just stop listening and tune out when I think my area is going to be threatened. I ignore the impact to the bigger-picture and focus on what I can control. I think that makes me a Separator, huh?"

We both nodded.

This dialogue was revealing the root of the real issues. As each individual owned up to their part, we felt the energy shift, and the discussion took on a completely different quality. Each person was more curious about their contribution to the situation than about focusing on what the other people had done wrong.

Mike spoke. "Well, I guess I have been enabling both of you," he said. "I tried to manage you in one-on-one meetings and never really focused on teamwork. I've been the Accommodator!"

"Isn't it funny how you have each been playing a role in defusing the tension, which undermined the potential for teamwork?" CrisMarie said. The three agreed.

Spending time on the ME and WE enables teams to more easily resolve business issues. Cooperation and creativity soars. Solutions emerge that weren't in anyone's mind prior to doing the ME and WE work.

We allowed other team members to spend time with the horses and receive critical feedback, then we moved back into the conference room. Sure enough, CAC made some creative shifts in their approach. They realized that overall business success depended on team alignment. It was important to keep the main business successful and to support these new lines of business that were just beginning. But, most importantly, they recognized how crucial team alignment is for success.

The first big move involved performance measures. The leadership team decided to forgo their functional business bonuses for bonuses based on overall CAC success. They called it "One Team, One Bonus!"

The second move was to treat these different businesses as unique entities that needed to incubate in order to grow. Each of the businesses was at a different stage, and each needed to be led and measured differently. The team decided to keep them in separate business units with unique business measures. The team didn't want to create large gaps between the main business and these other business units, so they set up a nine-month managerial rotation. Key mid-level managers would rotate between the main business and the other start-up businesses.

This strategy was hugely successful in the short term with the first new business line. The next two lines achieved success even more quickly. The leadership team stayed aligned and continued to lean into the oh, sh*t! moments to reap the value of teamwork. As we worked at other levels within the organization, focusing on improving teamwork and *using conflict* skills, we were excited to witness the level of engagement driving innovative problem solving across the organization. The company's gross revenue just two years later when we finished our engagement was more than $500 million.

DESIGNING THEIR WAY TO CREATIVITY

We worked with an architectural design firm that ran head-on into similar issues. The firm's founders were Valerie and Wilson (a couple) and Valerie's best friend, Jodi. Valerie was the CEO, and her focus was design. Wilson was the architect, and Jodi was the CFO. The business had grown steadily for eight years, and they were hitting more than $15 million in revenue with just ten employees. The three-year goal was to hit $20 million. One year into that goal, revenue stalled. Jodi asked us to do a strategic off-site for the company.

In our first conversation, Jodi revealed that the business had actually begun losing money. Jodi thought the company needed a strategic off-site to sort things out, but the real issue was an increasing gap between Valerie and Wilson. Jodi did not know how to handle it. She brought Valerie and Wilson to the off-site saying they needed a strategic session to reignite inspiration and get back on track to hit the $20 million goal.

During the off-site, the team revealed that six months prior, Valerie had landed a contract with a high-end intentional-living community. This was right up Valerie's alley. She was passionate about the project and believed everyone was on board, driving for that $20 million goal. By the time of the off-site, though, the project's profit margin was eroding. Jodi went through the numbers and shared how much was being spent in architect fees. Valerie exploded.

"What?" she nearly yelled. "Wilson, why are we paying other architects when you are doing the job?"

"Look, I'm doing the best I can," he shot back. "I needed help. Back off!"

We were smack dab in the middle of the team's, the couple's, and the business's oh, sh*t! moment.

The easy button at that point would have been to follow the blame game: It's Wilson's fault for not working hard enough. It's Valerie's fault for picking such a big project without buy-in from the rest of the team. It's Jodi's fault for not addressing the money issue sooner.

Any one of these rabbit holes could have eaten up lots of time and maybe even generated a solution, but the team would not likely discover the best or most creative insights. We suggested a different route. Why not step away from problem-solving and instead go deeper into what was driving each person's decisions and behaviors. As we've shared, we believe the most effective path originates from a place of genuine curiosity, not from the right-wrong trap.

CrisMarie said, "Seems like Wilson's hiring of architectural resources took you by surprise, Valerie."

"Yes! I thought we were working this together. I didn't know he was outsourcing the whole thing!" Valerie was annoyed and hurt.

CrisMarie said, "Wilson, it might be helpful if you let Valerie know what drove your decision to hire other architects for this project."

Wilson turned to Valerie, "Listen, I tried to tell you before you signed on to this project: this is your passion, not mine. I've always wanted to do more commercial work. I've gone along as best as I could, but I've picked up some commercial projects of my own. So I hired people from another firm to do the work."

Valerie was crushed and still upset. "How did I not know?" she asked. "I always thought this is what we both—all of us—wanted. We worked so hard to create this direction."

Wilson was silent. Jodi looked on helplessly.

Valerie continued, "I don't know how to get through this. You want something I don't. We want such different things."

Valerie and Wilson faced differences that felt irreconcilable and could split the company apart. We encouraged them to hold off trying to solve the problem. We wanted to help them get unstuck from the creativity-killer trap and shift to access their collective potential.

The first step is to slow things down and not rush to a solution. Truly hearing someone else requires you to suspend the desire for the right solution. This is counterintuitive. Naturally, when there is a problem, we want to fix it. Fixing it is not always the best solution, but discussion is invariably the first and best step to reach a creative outcome.

When Valerie, Wilson, and Jodi were able to slow down and get curious, Wilson let Valerie know he was unhappy. He shared that he had never been in alignment with the new project. This caused some pain and concern, but Valerie let it in. She acknowledged that while she had heard his desire for something other than residential design, she thought the intentional community met his passion for commercial projects. And, she acknowledged that when she got the contract, she was so excited that she probably didn't listen when he said no.

By shifting focus from quick solution to what was driving each person's behaviors and actions, we got underneath to a better space for creative options and not just fixing problems.

Once the conversation got to the core of people's behavior and opened to vulnerability, curiosity, and new possibility, magic did happen!

Jodi remembered that the intentional community had talked about their own financial goals. They had brought Jodi in for a consult some months ago and were looking for commercial properties to invest in. The request for advice seemed separate and unrelated to the team's issue. Jodi never even considered talking to Wilson or Valerie about the meeting. But now as she listened, she connected the dots. The intentional community wanted to purchase commercial properties to redesign, upgrade, and rent or sell at a profit. Now, with everything out on the table, Jodi realized Wilson might be the perfect architect for their project.

The idea evolved into a win-win for everyone. Wilson met with the board of the intentional community and happily agreed to partner with them on its commercial projects. This architectural design firm hit $20 million six months ahead of schedule, and each of the founders was thrilled with the work they were doing!

When teams, even couples, are facing what feel like irreconcilable differences, sometimes the best, most creative solution will only emerge when they take a different approach. They must remain curious, or regain curiosity through conflict. In doing so, they step away from immediate problem-solving and slow down, listen, and get underneath the differences to find the creative gold.

SUMMING UP

Learning how and having the courage to use the energy of conflict during tough conversations can change business failure and business success. Whether it's a team of two people or twelve, being vulnerable and real (the ME) and being curious about the other by checking out your stories (the WE), are the raw ingredients that transform conflict into team brilliance. The focus shifts from my way or your way and opens possibilities for a whole new way. The magic is right at your fingertips, and it is free!

This system helps your team reach innovation and transformation; not just once, but repeatedly. A natural inspiration fuels you, the team, and the business. It's the catalyst that turns lead into gold, and the team awakens their creative genius. It's the very essence of what we call *collective creativity.* The experience is unmistakable. It feels expansive, exciting, and inspiring. Success and fulfillment abound, the bottom line grows. What will you choose: avoid or use?

People in business are always looking for the next big thing. We strongly believe that the next big thing isn't *out there*, it's within and between you and your people.

Nothing is more powerful and transformational than people working together and enhancing their relationships while reaching for phenomenal business results.

Simply put: you, me, and results matter. When we hold the tension that rises with that combination, magic happens. Don't settle for anything less on your team or in your business!

Try it. If you get stuck in the mess of conflict and want some help, give us a call. We'll work through the mess with you and your team, and help you develop the skills to regularly access innovative, creative solutions that build your team's competitive advantage!

BONUS MATERIAL

In this book, *The Beauty of Conflict: Harnessing Your Team's Competitive Advantage*, we include several tools.

We also wanted to provide you with additional support, so we've created FREE bonus material as a supplement to the tools outlined in the book. This bonus material includes additional tips, tools, and information that you can apply immediately for yourself, your team, and your organization.

To download the bonus material, go to:
www.Thriveinc.com/beautyofconflict/bonus

There you'll find:

- **OPT-OUT STYLE ASSESSMENT:** Want to know your Opt-Out Style? Take this assessment to learn how you can opt-out of conflict so that you can deal with conflict more effectively.

- **THE OH SH*T! KIT** (a ME tool) for when you're having an Oh Sh*t! moment:
    - your boss is driving you nuts
    - your teammate is rubbing you the wrong way
    - you can't find the words to express what you really feel

  This kit will give you the tools to take care of yourself in those Oh Sh*t! moments.

- **HOW TO HAVE TOUGH CONVERSATIONS AT WORK** (a WE tool). This is a step-by-step guide to help you prepare for, and successfully have, a tough conversation so you get the outcome you want.

- **MAKE YOUR MEETINGS MATTER** (a BUSINESS tool). This provides simple, practical and proven tools to get the most out of your team, your meeting, and your time.

ACKNOWLEDGEMENTS

We want to thank the awesome team of people who have helped us bring this book to the pages. The list of names is too long and we'd likely miss a few.

In short, we want to acknowledge our clients who have provided their stories—successes and failures—and been willing to opt in through it all.

We want to give a shout out to the many editors who have supported us through our writing process, be it blog posting or book chapters.

Also to the colleagues, friends and even family who have been willing to take the time to read and provide feedback to us along the way.

Finally, to our friends who remind us when we get discouraged or want to opt out that it is worth it to hang in.

We could not have done this without our tribe!

ENDNOTES

1. "Majority of U.S. Employees Not Engaged Despite Gains in 2014" *Gallup: Employee Engagement*, Amy Adkins, accessed January 28, 2015, www.gallup.com/poll/181289/majority-employees-not-engaged-despite-gains-2014.aspx

2. Roberts, Monty. *From My Hands To Yours: Lessons from a Lifetime of Training Championship Horses.* Monty and Pat Roberts Inc., 2007.

3. Roberts, Monty. *From My Hands To Yours: Lessons from a Lifetime of Training Championship Horses.* Monty and Pat Roberts Inc., 2007.

4. Bennet Wong and Jock McKeen, *The New Manual for Life* (Gabriola Island, British Columbia, Canada: PD Publishing, 1998), 63.

5. Ibid

6. Ibid

7. Ibid

8. Linda Kohanov, *Power of the Herd: A Nonpredatory Approach to Social Intelligence, Leadership and Innovation* (Novato: New World Library 2013) 25

9. Bob Sherwin, *Why Women Are More Effective Leaders Than Men* (Business Insider, January 24, 2014), www.businessinsider.com/study-women-are-better-leaders-2014-1

10. Jack Zenger and Joseph Folkman, *Are Women Better Leaders Than Men* (Harvard Business Review: March 15, 2012), https://hbr.org/2012/03/a-study-in-leadership-women-do

11. Adapted from, *The Haven Communication Model*, www.haven.ca/resource/model-haven-communication-model

12. Handel, Steven, *The Power of Being Heard: How Listening to Others Helps Empower Them* (The Emotion Machine, March 19, 2012), www.theemotionmachine.com/the-power-of-being-heard

13. Bruneau, Emile G. and Rebecca Saxe, *The Power of Being Heard*: The benefits of 'perspective-giving' in the context of intergroup conflict (Journal of Experimental Social Psychology. July 2012, Vol. 48(4)), www.sciencedirect.com/science/article/pii/S0022103112000297

14. Simon Sinek, *Start with Why: How Great Leaders Inspire Everyone to Take*

Action (New York: Penguin Group, 2009)

15. Jim Collins, Jerry I. Porras, *Built to Last: Successful Habits of Visionary Companies* (Harper Business Essentials, 2004) [4883]

16. Patrick Lencioni, *The Advantage: Why Organizational Health Trumps Everything Else in Business* (San Francisco: Jossey-Bass, A Wiley Imprint, 2012) pg. 77

17. Ibid.

18. Patrick Lencioni, *Death* by *Meeting, A Leadership Fable...About Solving the Most Painful Problem in Business* (San Francisco: Josey-Bass, a Wiley Imprint, 2004)

19. Edwards, Cliff. *Intel: Supercharging Silicon Valley* (Bloomberg 2004), www.bloomberg.com/news/articles/2004-10-03/intel-supercharging-silicon-valley

20. Harari, Oren. *Quotations from Chairman Powell: A Leadership Primer* (GovLeaders.org, 1996), www.govleaders.org/powell.htm

21. Vivian Giang, *The 'Two Pizza Rule' Is Jeff Bezos' Secret to Productive Meetings*, Business Insider, October 29, 2013, www.businessinsider.com/jeff-bezos-two-pizza-rule-for-productive-meetings-2013-10

22. Project Management Institute, "Why Good Strategies Fail, Lessons for the C-Suite" The Economist, March 2013

23. William Bridges, *Managing Transitions: Making the Most of Change* 2nd Edition (Boston: Da Capo Press a Member of the Perseus Books Group, 2003)

24. Elizabeth Kubler-Ross, M.D., *On Death & Dying: What the Dying Have to Teach Doctors, Nurses, Clergy & Their Own Families* (New York: Scribner, 1969)

INDEX

Made in the USA
San Bernardino, CA
29 December 2018